A PICTORIAL GOSPEL

ROGIER VAN DER WEYDEN (c. 1400–64)

LUKE MAKING A PORTRAIT OF THE VIRGIN

A PICTORIAL GOSPEL

A LIFE OF CHRIST

IN THE WORKS OF THE OLD MASTERS
AND THE WORDS OF THE GOSPELS

COMPILED BY
ELIOT HODGKIN

THE MACMILLAN COMPANY
NEW YORK
1950

THIS BOOK IS DEDICATED TO

MAXIE

FOR WHOM IT WAS STARTED

AND TO MIMI

WHO HELPED TO FINISH IT

Printed in Great Britain

INTRODUCTION

THIS book needs hardly any explanation. It brings together two things which are complementary but which have never before been combined with such completeness, the Gospel story and the works of art in which the old masters sought to illustrate it, my intention being that each should thereby gain fresh meaning and interest.

The life of Christ is told, on the left-hand pages, in the words of the New Testament. Incidents from the four Gospels have been combined to form a consecutive narrative. Practically all recorded incidents of Christ's life have been included, and much of his teaching. The text is arranged in chronological order so far as I could ascertain it, but in this connection there are a number of points about which scholars do not agree. The Authorized Version has been used, with the following differences: the narrative is not broken up into numbered verses; quotation marks are used to denote direct speech; and Old Testament names are given their more familiar forms, i.e. Elijah for Elias, etc. The text of the Authorised Version is Crown Copyright, and is used by permission.

The right-hand pages are devoted to illustrations of the page opposite. These include paintings and drawings of all schools and periods, ranging from the anonymous illustrators of medieval manuscripts to Blake and Ford Madox Brown. They come from galleries, museums and private collections all over the world; and while some are well known others have never before been reproduced, or only in costly and inaccessible works of scholarship. Some, such as the drawings from the Codex Aureus in the Escorial Library, have been photographed specially for this book.

In choosing the pictures, I have been guided by three considerations: that they should illustrate the text, should have genuine artistic merit, and should not be over-familiar. Although I cannot pretend that I have always succeeded in fulfilling all three conditions, I think I can claim that they include a high proportion of unfamiliar works.

In obtaining the illustrations for this book, I have experienced remarkable kindness and co-operation from the directors and staff of museums and galleries, and from collectors generally: unfortunately, their names are too numerous to mention here, but I would like to express my gratitude. The help I have received from the Warburg Institute, however, has been so exceptionally generous that I cannot forbear to mention it by name.

THE ILLUSTRATIONS

[7]

ACKNOWLEDGEMENTS

A. C. L., Brussels: 47 51 99 135 155 161 169

Alinari, Florence: 23 29 39 55a 59 67 75a 87 93a 97 109 125 131 139 143a 151 153 159 171 183a 187 205a

Anderson, Rome: 25 43 77 91a 165 191 211

T. & R. Annan & Sons, Glasgow: 91b 119

British Council: 193

Bruckmann, Munich: 103 147

Bulloz, Paris: 11 49 65 149a 203

Caisse Nationale des Monuments Historiques, Paris: 35 79

Cleveland Museum of Art, Ohio: 15

R. B. Fleming & Co., London: 69

Giraudon, Paris: 137 185

Hanfstaengl, Munich: 181

Photo Mas, Barcelona: 95

Ministry of Works, London: 57 85 117a 201

Maurice Moullet, Fribourg: 53a 123

National Gallery, London: 179

Photostudios, London: 71

Rijksmuseum, Amsterdam: 31a

E. Serrano, A.F.C.A., Madrid: 75b 129

Wolfrum, Vienna: 33

Museum Photographs: Frontispiece, 13 17 19 21 27 31b 37 41 45 53b 55b 61a-b-c 63 73 81 83 89 93b 101 105a-b 107 111a-b 113 115 117b 121 127a-b 133 141b 143b 145 149b 157 163 167 173 175 177 183b 189 195 197 199 205b 207 209 212

THE BEGINNING

THE beginning of the gospel of Jesus Christ, the Son of God.

ST MARK I (I)

IN the beginning was the Word, and the Word was with God, and the Word was God. The same was in the beginning with God. All things were made by him; and without him was not any thing made that was made. In him was life; and the life was the light of men. And the light shineth in darkness; and the darkness comprehended it not.

ST JOHN I (I–5)

MATTHEW WRITING FROM THE ANGEL'S DICTATION

THERE was in the days of Herod, the king of Judæa, a certain priest named Zacharias, of the course of Abia: and his wife was of the daughters of Aaron, and her name was Elisabeth. And they were both righteous before God, walking in all the commandments and ordinances of the Lord blameless. And they had no child, because that Elisabeth was barren, and they both were now well stricken in years.

And it came to pass, that while he executed the priest's office before God in the order of his course, according to the custom of the priest's office, his lot was to burn incense when he went into the temple of the Lord. And the whole multitude of the people were praying without at the time of incense. And there appeared unto him an angel of the Lord standing on the right side of the altar of incense. And when Zacharias saw him, he was troubled, and fear fell upon him. But the angel said unto him: "Fear not, Zacharias: for thy prayer is heard; and thy wife Elisabeth shall bear thee a son, and thou shalt call his name John. And thou shalt have joy and gladness; and many shall rejoice at his birth. For he shall be great in the sight of the Lord, and shall drink neither wine nor strong drink; and he shall be filled with the Holy Ghost, even from his mother's womb. And many of the children of Israel shall he turn to the Lord their God." And he shall go before him in the spirit and power of Elijah, to turn the hearts of the fathers to the children, and the disobedient to the wisdom of the just; to make ready a people prepared for the Lord."

And Zacharias said unto the angel:—"Whereby shall I know this? for I am an old man, and my wife well stricken in years." And the angel answering said unto him:—"I am Gabriel, that stand in the presence of God; and am sent to speak unto thee, and to shew thee these glad tidings. And, behold, thou shalt be dumb, and not able to speak, until the day that these things shall be performed, because thou believest not my words, which shall be fulfilled in their season."

And the people waited for Zacharias, and marvelled that he tarried so long in the temple. And when he came out, he could not speak unto them: and they perceived that he had seen a vision in the temple: for he beckoned unto them, and remained speechless. And it came to pass, that, as soon as the days of his ministration were accomplished, he departed to his own house.

And after those days his wife Elisabeth conceived, and hid herself five months, saying, Thus hath the Lord dealt with me in the days wherein he looked on me, to take away my reproach among men.

ST LUKE I (5–25)

BERNER NELKENMEISTER (End of XV Century)   *Berner Kunstmuseum*

THE ANGEL GABRIEL WITH ZACHARIAS

A N D in the sixth month the angel Gabriel was sent from God unto a city of Galilee, named Nazareth, to a virgin espoused to a man whose name was Joseph, of the house of David; and the virgin's name was Mary. And the angel came in unto her, and said:—

"Hail, thou that art highly favoured, the Lord is with thee: blessed art thou among women."

And when she saw him, she was troubled at his saying, and cast in her mind what manner of salutation this should be. And the angel said unto her:—

"Fear not, Mary: for thou hast found favour with God. And, behold, thou shalt conceive in thy womb, and bring forth a son, and shalt call his name JESUS. He shall be great, and shall be called the Son of the Highest: and the Lord God shall give unto him the throne of his father David; and he shall reign over the house of Jacob for ever; and of his kingdom there shall be no end."

Then said Mary unto the angel:—"How shall this be, seeing I know not a man?" And the angel answered and said unto her:—

"The Holy Ghost shall come upon thee, and the power of the Highest shall overshadow thee: therefore also that holy thing which shall be born of thee shall be called the Son of God. And, behold, thy cousin Elisabeth, she hath also conceived a son in her old age: and this is the sixth month with her, who was called barren. For with God nothing shall be impossible."

And Mary said:—"Behold the handmaid of the Lord; be it unto me according to thy word." And the angel departed from her.

ST LUKE I (26–38)

EL GRECO (1548–1625)   *Courtesy of Mr. Ralph M. Coe, Cleveland, Ohio*

THE ANNUNCIATION

AND Mary arose in those days, and went into the hill country with haste, into a city of Judah; and entered into the house of Zacharias, and saluted Elisabeth. And it came to pass, that, when Elisabeth heard the salutation of Mary, the babe leaped in her womb; and Elisabeth was filled with the Holy Ghost: and she spake out with a loud voice, and said:—"Blessed art thou among women, and blessed is the fruit of thy womb. And whence is this to me, that the mother of my Lord should come to me? For, lo, as soon as the voice of thy salutation sounded in mine ears, the babe leaped in my womb for joy. And blessed is she that believed: for there shall be a performance of those things which were told her from the Lord." And Mary said:—

"My soul doth magnify the Lord, and my spirit hath rejoiced in God my Saviour. For he hath regarded the low estate of his handmaiden: For behold, from henceforth all generations shall call me blessed. For he that is mighty hath done to me great things; And holy is his name. And his mercy is on them that fear him from generation to generation. He hath shewed strength with his arm; he hath scattered the proud in the imagination of their hearts. He hath put down the mighty from their seats, and exalted them of low degree. He hath filled the hungry with good things; and the rich he hath sent empty away. He hath holpen his servant Israel, in remembrance of his mercy; as he spake to our fathers, to Abraham, and to his seed for ever."

And Mary abode with her about three months, and returned to her own house.

ST LUKE I (39–56)

BARTHOLOMAUS ZEITBLOM
(c. 1455–c. 1520)

THE VISITATION

THE BIRTH AND NAMING OF JOHN THE BAPTIST

NOW Elisabeth's full time came that she should be delivered; and she brought forth a son. And her neighbours and her cousins heard how the Lord had shewed great mercy upon her; and they rejoiced with her. And it came to pass, that on the eighth day they came to circumcise the child; and they called him Zacharias, after the name of his father. And his mother answered and said:—"Not so; but he shall be called John." And they said unto her:—"There is none of thy kindred that is called by this name." And they made signs to his father, how he would have him called. And he asked for a writing table, and wrote, saying:—"His name is John." And they marvelled all. And his mouth was opened immediately, and his tongue loosed, and he spake, and praised God. And fear came on all that dwelt round about them: and all these sayings were noised abroad throughout all the hill country of Judæa. And all they that heard them laid them up in their hearts, saying, "What manner of child shall this be!" And the hand of the Lord was with him.

ST LUKE I (57–66)

THE PROPHECY OF ZACHARIAS

AND his father Zacharias was filled with the Holy Ghost, and prophesied, saying:—

"Blessed be the Lord God of Israel; for he hath visited and redeemed his people, and hath raised up an horn of salvation for us in the house of his servant David; as he spake by the mouth of his holy prophets, which have been since the world began: That we should be saved from our enemies, and from the hand of all that hate us; to perform the mercy promised to our fathers, and to remember his holy covenant; the oath which he sware to our father Abraham, that he would grant unto us, that we being delivered out of the hand of our enemies might serve him without fear, in holiness and righteousness before him, all the days of our life. And thou, child, shalt be called the prophet of the Highest: for thou shalt go before the face of the Lord to prepare his ways; to give knowledge of salvation unto his people by the remission of their sins, through the tender mercy of our God; whereby the dayspring from on high hath visited us, to give light to them that sit in darkness and in the shadow of death, to guide our feet into the way of peace."

And the child grew, and waxed strong in spirit, and was in the deserts till the day of his shewing unto Israel.

ST LUKE I (67–80)

GIOVANNI DI PAOLO (c. 1403-1482)   *National Gallery, London*

THE NAMING OF THE BAPTIST

N O W the birth of JESUS CHRIST was on this wise:—

When as his mother Mary was espoused to Joseph, before they came together, she was found with child of the Holy Ghost. Then Joseph her husband, being a just man, and not willing to make her a publick example, was minded to put her away privily. But while he thought on these things, behold, the angel of the Lord appeared unto him in a dream, saying:— "Joseph, thou son of David, fear not to take unto thee Mary thy wife: for that which is conceived in her is of the Holy Ghost. And she shall bring forth a son, and thou shalt call his name JESUS: for he shall save his people from their sins." Now all this was done, that it might be fulfilled which was spoken of the Lord by the prophet, saying:—Behold, a virgin shall be with child, and shall bring forth a son, and they shall call his name Emmanuel, which being interpreted is, God with us.

Then Joseph being raised from sleep did as the angel of the Lord had bidden him, and took unto him his wife: and knew her not till she had brought forth her firstborn son: and he called his name JESUS.

ST MATTHEW I (18–25)

A N D it came to pass in those days, that there went out a decree from Cæsar Augustus, that all the world should be taxed. (This taxing was first made when Cyrenius was governor of Syria.) And all went to be taxed, every one into his own city. And Joseph also went up from Galilee, out of the city of Nazareth, into Judæa, unto the city of David, which is called Bethlehem; (because he was of the house and lineage of David;) to be taxed with Mary his espoused wife, being great with child. And so it was, that, while they were there, the days were accomplished that she should be delivered. And she brought forth her firstborn son, and wrapped him in swaddling clothes, and laid him in a manger; because there was no room for them in the inn.

ST LUKE II (1–7)

GEERTGEN TOT SINT JANS (Late XV Century)   *National Gallery, London*

THE NATIVITY, AT NIGHT

AND there were in the same country shepherds abiding in the field, keeping watch over their flock by night. And, lo, the angel of the Lord came upon them, and the glory of the Lord shone round about them: and they were sore afraid. And the angel said unto them:—"Fear not: for, behold, I bring you good tidings of great joy, which shall be to all people. For unto you is born this day in the city of David a Saviour, which is Christ the Lord. And this shall be a sign unto you; Ye shall find the babe wrapped in swaddling clothes, lying in a manger."

And suddenly there was with the angel a multitude of the heavenly host praising God, and saying:—Glory to God in the highest, and on earth peace, good will toward men. And it came to pass, as the angels were gone away from them into heaven, the shepherds said one to another:—"Let us now go even unto Bethlehem, and see this thing which is come to pass, which the Lord hath made known unto us." And they came with haste, and found Mary, and Joseph, and the babe lying in a manger. And when they had seen it, they made known abroad the saying which was told them concerning this child. And all they that heard it wondered at those things which were told them by the shepherds. But Mary kept all these things, and pondered them in her heart. And the shepherds returned, glorifying and praising God for all the things that they had heard and seen, as it was told unto them.

ST LUKE II (8–20)

HUGO VAN DER GOES (Died 1482)   *Uffizi, Florence*

ANGELS AND SHEPHERDS IN ADORATION

THE CIRCUMCISION AND PRESENTATION IN THE TEMPLE

AND when eight days were accomplished for the circumcising of the child, his name was called JESUS, which was so named of the angel before he was conceived in the womb.

And when the days of her purification according to the law of Moses were accomplished, they brought him to Jerusalem, to present him to the Lord; (as it is written in the law of the Lord, Every male that openeth the womb shall be called holy to the Lord); and to offer a sacrifice according to that which is said in the law of the Lord—a pair of turtledoves, or two young pigeons.

ST LUKE II (21–24)

SIMEON'S PRAYER

AND, behold, there was a man in Jerusalem, whose name was Simeon; and the same man was just and devout, waiting for the consolation of Israel: and the Holy Ghost was upon him. And it was revealed unto him by the Holy Ghost, that he should not see death, before he had seen the Lord's Christ. And he came by the Spirit into the temple: and when the parents brought in the child Jesus, to do for him after the custom of the law, then took he him up in his arms, and blessed God, and said:—"Lord, now lettest thou thy servant depart in peace according to thy word, for mine eyes have seen thy salvation, which thou hast prepared before the face of all people; a light to lighten the Gentiles, and the glory of thy people Israel; and Joseph and his mother marvelled at those things which were spoken of him. And Simeon blessed them, and said unto Mary his mother:—"Behold, this child is set for the fall and rising again of many in Israel; And for a sign which shall be spoken against; (Yea, a sword shall pierce through thy own soul also,) that the thoughts of many hearts may be revealed." And there was one Anna, a prophetess, the daughter of Phanuel, of the tribe of Aser: she was of a great age, and had lived with an husband seven years from her virginity: and she was a widow of about fourscore and four years, which departed not from the temple, but served God with fastings and prayers night and day. And she coming in that instant gave thanks likewise unto the Lord, and spake of him to all them that looked for redemption in Jerusalem.

ST LUKE II (25–38)

MANTEGNA (1431–1506)   (A detail from "The Circumcision of Jesus")   *Uffizi, Florence*

THE CIRCUMCISION

N O W when Jesus was born in Bethlehem of Judæa in the days of Herod the king, behold, there came wise men from the east to Jerusalem, saying:— "Where is he that is born King of the Jews? for we have seen his star in the east, and are come to worship him." When Herod the king had heard these things, he was troubled, and all Jerusalem with him. And when he had gathered all the chief priests and scribes of the people together, he demanded of them where Christ should be born. And they said unto him:—"In Bethlehem of Judæa: for thus it is written by the prophet, And thou Bethlehem, in the land of Judah, art not the least among the princes of Judah: For out of thee shall come a Governor, that shall rule my people Israel."

Then Herod, when he had privily called the wise men, inquired of them diligently what time the star appeared. And he sent them to Bethlehem, and said:—"Go and search diligently for the young child; and when ye have found him, bring me word again, that I may come and worship him also." When they had heard the king, they departed; and, lo, the star, which they saw in the east, went before them, till it came and stood over where the young child was. When they saw the star, they rejoiced with exceeding great joy. And when they were come into the house, they saw the young child with Mary his mother, and fell down, and worshipped him: and when they had opened their treasures, they presented unto him gifts; gold, and frankincense, and myrrh. And being warned of God in a dream that they should not return to Herod, they departed into their own country another way.

ST MATTHEW II (1–12)

GERARD DAVID (Active 1484; died 1523)   *National Gallery, London*

THE ADORATION OF THE KINGS

THE FLIGHT INTO EGYPT

AND when they were departed, behold, the angel of the Lord appeareth to Joseph in a dream, saying:—"Arise, and take the young child and his mother, and flee into Egypt, and be thou there until I bring thee word: for Herod will seek the young child to destroy him." When he arose, he took the young child and his mother by night, and departed into Egypt: and was there until the death of Herod: that it might be fulfilled which was spoken of the Lord by the prophet, saying:—Out of Egypt have I called my son.

ST MATTHEW II (13–15)

THE MASSACRE OF THE INNOCENTS

THEN Herod, when he saw that he was mocked of the wise men, was exceeding wroth, and sent forth, and slew all the children that were in Bethlehem, and in all the coasts thereof, from two years old and under, according to the time which he had diligently inquired of the wise men. Then was fulfilled that which was spoken by Jeremy the prophet, saying:—In Rama was there a voice heard, lamentation, and weeping, and great mourning, Rachel weeping for her children, and would not be comforted, because they are not.

ST MATTHEW II (16–18)

THE RETURN FROM EGYPT

BUT when Herod was dead, behold an angel of the Lord appeareth in a dream to Joseph in Egypt, saying:—"Arise, and take the young child and his mother, and go into the land of Israel: for they are dead which sought the young child's life." And he arose, and took the young child and his mother, and came into the land of Israel. But when he heard that Archelaus did reign in Judæa in the room of his father Herod, he was afraid to go thither: notwithstanding, being warned of God in a dream, he turned aside into the parts of Galilee: and he came and dwelt in a city called Nazareth: that it might be fulfilled which was spoken by the prophets:—He shall be called a Nazarene.

ST MATTHEW II (19–23)

GIOTTO (1266–1337)   *Arena Chapel, Padua*

THE MASSACRE OF THE INNOCENTS

A N D the child grew, and waxed strong in spirit, filled with wisdom: and the grace of God was upon him.

Now his parents went to Jerusalem every year at the feast of the passover. And when he was twelve years old, they went up to Jerusalem after the custom of the feast. And when they had fulfilled the days, as they returned, the child Jesus tarried behind in Jerusalem; and Joseph and his mother knew not of it. But they, supposing him to have been in the company, went a day's journey; and they sought him among their kinsfolk and acquaintance. And when they found him not, they turned back again to Jerusalem, seeking him. And it came to pass, that after three days they found him in the temple, sitting in the midst of the doctors, both hearing them, and asking them questions. And all that heard him were astonished at his understanding and answers.

And when they saw him, they were amazed: and his mother said unto him:—"Son, why hast thou thus dealt with us? behold, thy father and I have sought thee sorrowing." And he said unto them:—"How is it that ye sought me? wist ye not that I must be about my Father's business?" And they understood not the saying which he spake unto them.

And he went down with them, and came to Nazareth, and was subject unto them: but his mother kept all these sayings in her heart.

And Jesus increased in wisdom and stature, and in favour with God and man.

ST LUKE II (40–52)

RIBERA (1588–1652)   *Kunsthistorisches Museum, Vienna*

THE CHILD JESUS WITH THE DOCTORS

REMBRANDT (1607–69)   *From an etching in the British Museum*

THE RETURN TO NAZARETH

THE PREACHING OF JOHN THE BAPTIST

IN those days came John the Baptist, preaching in the wilderness of Judæa, and saying:—"Repent ye: for the kingdom of heaven is at hand. For this is he that was spoken of by the prophet Isaiah, saying:—The voice of one crying in the wilderness, prepare ye the way of the Lord, make his paths straight." And the same John had his raiment of camel's hair, and a leathern girdle about his loins; and his meat was locusts and wild honey. Then went out to him Jerusalem, and all Judæa, and all the region round about Jordan, and were baptized of him in Jordan, confessing their sins. But when he saw many of the Pharisees and Sadducees come to his baptism, he said unto them:— "O generation of vipers, who hath warned you to flee from the wrath to come? Bring forth therefore fruits meet for repentance: and think not to say within yourselves, We have Abraham to our father: for I say unto you, that God is able of these stones to raise up children unto Abraham. And now also the axe is laid unto the root of the trees: therefore every tree which bringeth not forth good fruit is hewn down, and cast into the fire. I indeed baptize you with water unto repentance: but he that cometh after me is mightier than I, whose shoes I am not worthy to bear: he shall baptize you with the Holy Ghost, and with fire: whose fan is in his hand, and he will throughly purge his floor, and gather his wheat into the garner; but he will burn up the chaff with unquenchable fire."

ST MATTHEW III (1–12)

THE BAPTISM OF JESUS

THEN cometh Jesus from Galilee to Jordan unto John, to be baptized of him. But John forbad him, saying:—"I have need to be baptized of thee, and comest Thou to me?" And Jesus answering said unto him:—"Suffer it to be so now: for thus it becometh us to fulfil all righteousness." Then he suffered him. And Jesus, when he was baptized, went up straightway out of the water: and, lo, the heavens were opened unto him, and he saw the Spirit of God descending like a dove, and lighting upon him: and lo a voice from heaven, saying:— This is my beloved Son, in whom I am well pleased.

ST MATTHEW III (13–17)

PATINIR (c. 1480–1524)   *Kunsthistorisches Museum, Vienna*

THE BAPTISM OF JESUS

AND Jesus being full of the Holy Ghost returned from Jordan, and was led by the Spirit into the wilderness, being forty days tempted of the devil. And in those days he did eat nothing: and when they were ended, he afterward hungered. And the devil said unto him:—"If thou be the Son of God, command this stone that it be made bread." And Jesus answered him, saying:— "It is written that man shall not live by bread alone, but by every word of God." And the devil, taking him up into an high mountain, shewed unto him all the kingdoms of the world in a moment of time. And the devil said unto him:—"All this power will I give thee, and the glory of them: for that is delivered unto me; and to whomsoever I will I give it. If thou therefore wilt worship me, all shall be thine." And Jesus answered and said unto him:—

"Get thee behind me, Satan: for it is written, thou shalt worship the Lord thy God, and him only shalt thou serve." And he brought him to Jerusalem, and set him on a pinnacle of the temple, and said unto him:—"If thou be the Son of God, cast thyself down from hence: for it is written, He shall give his angels charge over thee, to keep thee: and in their hands they shall bear thee up, lest at any time thou dash thy foot against a stone." And Jesus answering said unto him:—"It is said, Thou shalt not tempt the Lord thy God." And when the devil had ended all the temptation, he departed from him for a season.

ST LUKE IV (1–13)

POL DE LIMBOURG (Born c. 1380)
and his brothers

THE TEMPTATION OF JESUS

AGAIN the next day after John stood, and two of his disciples; and looking upon Jesus as he walked, he saith:—"Behold the Lamb of God." And the two disciples heard him speak, and they followed Jesus. Then Jesus turned, and saw them following, and saith unto them:—"What seek ye?" They said unto him:—"Rabbi, (which is to say, being interpreted, Master,) where dwellest thou?" He saith unto them:—"Come and see." They came and saw where he dwelt, and abode with him that day: for it was about the tenth hour. One of the two which heard John speak, and followed him, was Andrew, Simon Peter's brother. He first findeth his own brother Simon, and saith unto him:—"We have found the Messiah," which is, being interpreted, the Christ. And he brought him to Jesus. And when Jesus beheld him, he said:—"Thou art Simon the son of Jona: thou shalt be called Cephas," which is by interpretation, 'A stone.'

The day following Jesus would go forth into Galilee, and findeth Philip, and saith unto him:—"Follow me." Now Philip was of Bethsaida, the city of Andrew and Peter. Philip findeth Nathanael, and saith unto him:—"We have found him, of whom Moses in the law, and the prophets, did write, Jesus of Nazareth, the son of Joseph." And Nathanael said unto him:—"Can there any good thing come out of Nazareth?" Philip saith unto him:—"Come and see." Jesus saw Nathanael coming to him, and saith of him:—"Behold an Israelite indeed, in whom is no guile!" Nathanael saith unto him:—"Whence knowest thou me?" Jesus answered and said unto him:—"Before that Philip called thee, when thou wast under the fig tree, I saw thee." Nathanael answered and saith unto him:—"Rabbi, thou art the Son of God; thou art the King of Israel." Jesus answered and said unto him:—"Because I said unto thee, I saw thee under the fig tree, believest thou? thou shalt see greater things than these." And he saith unto him:—"Verily, verily, I say unto you, hereafter ye shall see heaven open, and the angels of God ascending and descending upon the Son of Man."

ST JOHN I (35–51)

THE MASTER OF ST. JOHN'S ALTAR (Second half of XV Century)   *Courtesy of the John G. Johnson Collection, Philadelphia*

("St. John Preaching, Christ and Disciples")

JOHN AND JESUS WITH THEIR DISCIPLES

THE MARRIAGE AT CANA

AND the third day there was a marriage in Cana of Galilee; and the mother of Jesus was there: and both Jesus was called, and his disciples, to the marriage. And when they wanted wine, the mother of Jesus saith unto him:—"They have no wine." Jesus saith unto her:—"Woman, what have I to do with thee? Mine hour is not yet come." His mother saith unto the servants:—"Whatsoever he saith unto you, do it." And there were set there six waterpots of stone, after the manner of the purifying of the Jews, containing two or three firkins apiece. Jesus saith unto them:—"Fill the waterpots with water." And they filled them up to the brim. And he saith unto them:—"Draw out now, and bear unto the governor of the feast." And they bare it. When the ruler of the feast had tasted the water that was made wine, and knew not whence it was, (but the servants which drew the water knew) the governor of the feast called the bridegroom, and saith unto him:—"Every man at the beginning doth set forth good wine; and when men have well drunk, then that which is worse: but thou hast kept the good wine until now." This beginning of miracles did Jesus in Cana of Galilee, and manifested forth his glory; and his disciples believed on him.

After this he went down to Capernaum, he, and his mother, and his brethren, and his disciples: and they continued there not many days.

ST JOHN II (1–12)

GERARD DAVID (Active 1484; died 1523) Louvre, Paris

THE MARRIAGE AT CANA

AND the Jews' passover was at hand, and Jesus went up to Jerusalem, and found in the temple those that sold oxen and sheep and doves, and the changers of money sitting: and when he had made a scourge of small cords, he drove them all out of the temple, and the sheep, and the oxen; and poured out the changers' money, and overthrew the tables: and said unto them that sold doves:—"Take these things hence; make not my Father's house an house of merchandise." And his disciples remembered that it was written:—The zeal of thine house hath eaten me up. Then answered the Jews and said unto him:—"What sign shewest thou unto us, seeing that thou doest these things?" Jesus answered and said unto them:—"Destroy this temple, and in three days I will raise it up." Then said the Jews:—"Forty and six years was this temple in building, and wilt Thou rear it up in three days?" But he spake of the temple of his body. When therefore he was risen from the dead, his disciples remembered that he had said this unto them; and they believed the scripture, and the word which Jesus had said.

Now when he was in Jerusalem at the passover, in the feast day, many believed in his name, when they saw the miracles which he did. But Jesus did not commit himself unto them, because he knew all men, and needed not that any should testify of man: for he knew what was in man.

ST JOHN II (13–25)

CHRIST DRIVING THE MONEY-CHANGERS FROM THE TEMPLE

THERE was a man of the Pharisees, named Nicodemus, a ruler of the Jews: the same came to Jesus by night, and said unto him:—"Rabbi, we know that thou art a teacher come from God: for no man can do these miracles that thou doest, except God be with him." Jesus answered and said unto him:— "Verily, verily, I say unto thee, except a man be born again, he cannot see the kingdom of God." Nicodemus saith unto him:—"How can a man be born when he is old? can he enter the second time into his mother's womb, and be born?" Jesus answered:—"Verily, verily, I say unto thee, except a man be born of water and of the Spirit he cannot enter into the kingdom of God. That which is born of the flesh is flesh: and that which is born of the Spirit is spirit. Marvel not that I said unto thee, ye must be born again. The wind bloweth where it listeth, and thou hearest the sound thereof, but canst not tell whence it cometh, and whither it goeth: so is every one that is born of the Spirit." Nicodemus answered and said unto him:—"How can these things be?" Jesus answered and said unto him:—"Art thou a master of Israel, and knowest not these things? Verily, verily, I say unto thee, We speak that we do know, and testify that we have seen; and ye receive not our witness. If I have told you earthly things, and ye believe not, how shall ye believe, if I tell you of heavenly things? And no man hath ascended up to heaven, but he that came down from heaven, even the Son of man which is in heaven. And as Moses lifted up the serpent in the wilderness, even so must the Son of man be lifted up: that whosoever believeth in him should not perish, but have eternal life.

"For God so loved the world, that he gave his only begotten Son, that whosoever believeth in him should not perish, but have everlasting life. For God sent not his Son into the world to condemn the world; but that the world through him might be saved. He that believeth on him is not condemned: but he that believeth not is condemned already, because he hath not believed in the name of the only begotten Son of God. And this is the condemnation, that light is come into the world, and men loved darkness rather than light, because their deeds were evil. For every one that doeth evil hateth the light, neither cometh to the light, lest his deeds should be reproved. But he that doeth truth cometh to the light, that his deeds may be made manifest, that they are wrought in God."

ST JOHN III (1–21)

[42]

TINTORETTO (1518–88)   ("The Chastisement with Serpents")   *Scuola di S. Rocco, Venice*

MOSES LIFTING UP THE SERPENT IN THE WILDERNESS

HEROD IMPRISONS JOHN THE BAPTIST

BUT Herod the tetrarch, being reproved by him for Herodias his brother Philip's wife, and for all the evils which Herod had done, added yet this above all, that he shut up John in prison.

ST LUKE III (19–20)

JESUS HEALS THE NOBLEMAN'S SON

NOW after two days he departed thence, and went into Galilee. For Jesus himself testified, that a prophet hath no honour in his own country. Then when he was come into Galilee, the Galilæans received him, having seen all the things that he did at Jerusalem at the feast: for they also went unto the feast.

So Jesus came again into Cana of Galilee, where he made the water wine. And there was a certain nobleman, whose son was sick at Capernaum. When he heard that Jesus was come out of Judæa into Galilee, he went unto him, and besought him that he would come down, and heal his son: for he was at the point of death. Then said Jesus unto him:—"Except ye see signs and wonders, ye will not believe." The nobleman saith unto him, "Sir, come down ere my child die." Jesus saith unto him:—"Go thy way; thy son liveth." And the man believed the word that Jesus had spoken unto him, and he went his way. And as he was now going down, his servants met him, and told him, saying, "Thy son liveth." Then inquired he of them the hour when he began to amend. And they said unto him:—"Yesterday at the seventh hour the fever left him." So the father knew that it was at the same hour, in the which Jesus said unto him, "Thy son liveth": and himself believed, and his whole house. This is again the second miracle that Jesus did when he was come out of Judæa into Galilee.

ST JOHN IV (43–54)

HANS FRIES (1460–1518)   *Kunstmuseum, Basel*

JOHN THE BAPTIST REPROVING HEROD

AND he came to Nazareth, where he had been brought up: and, as his custom was, he went into the synagogue on the sabbath day, and stood up for to read. And there was delivered unto him the book of the prophet Isaiah. And when he had opened the book, he found the place where it was written:—The Spirit of the Lord is upon me, because he hath anointed me to preach the gospel to the poor; he hath sent me to heal the brokenhearted, to preach deliverance to the captives, and recovering of sight to the blind, to set at liberty them that are bruised, to preach the acceptable year of the Lord. And he closed the book, and he gave it again to the minister, and sat down. And the eyes of all them that were in the synagogue were fastened on him. And he began to say unto them:—"This day is this scripture fulfilled in your ears." And all bare him witness, and wondered at the gracious words which proceeded out of his mouth. And they said:—"Is not this Joseph's son?" And he said unto them:—"Ye will surely say unto me this proverb, Physician, heal thyself: whatsoever we have heard done in Capernaum, do also here in thy country." And he said:—"Verily I say unto you, No prophet is accepted in his own country. But I tell you of a truth, many widows were in Israel in the days of Elijah, when the heaven was shut up three years and six months, when great famine was throughout all the land; but unto none of them was Elijah sent, save unto Sarepta, a city of Sidon, unto a woman that was a widow. And many lepers were in Israel in the time of Elisha the prophet; and none of them was cleansed, saving Naaman the Syrian." And all they in the synagogue, when they heard these things, were filled with wrath, and rose up, and thrust him out of the city, and led him unto the brow of the hill whereon their city was built, that they might cast him down headlong. But he passing through the midst of them went his way.

ST LUKE IV (16–30)

DIERIC BOUTS (1400?–75)   *St Pierre, Louvain*

ELIJAH IN THE WILDERNESS

WHEN therefore the Lord knew how the Pharisees had heard that Jesus made and baptized more disciples than John, (though Jesus himself baptized not, but his disciples) he left Judæa, and departed again into Galilee. And he must needs go through Samaria. Then cometh he to a city of Samaria, which is called Sychar, near to the parcel of ground that Jacob gave to his son Joseph. Now Jacob's well was there. Jesus therefore, being wearied with his journey, sat thus on the well: and it was about the sixth hour. There cometh a woman of Samaria to draw water: Jesus saith unto her:—"Give me to drink." (For his disciples were gone away unto the city to buy meat.) Then saith the woman of Samaria unto him:—"How is it that thou, being a Jew, askest drink of me, which am a woman of Samaria? for the Jews have no dealings with the Samaritans." Jesus answered and said unto her:—"If thou knewest the gift of God, and who it is that saith to thee, give me to drink; thou wouldest have asked of him, and he would have given thee living water."

The woman saith unto him:—"Sir, thou hast nothing to draw with, and the well is deep: from whence then hast thou that living water? Art thou greater than our father Jacob, which gave us the well, and drank thereof himself, and his children, and his cattle?" Jesus answered and said unto her:—"Whosoever drinketh of this water shall thirst again: but whosoever drinketh of the water that I shall give him shall never thirst; but the water that I shall give him shall be in him a well of water springing up into everlasting life." The woman saith unto him:—"Sir, give me this water, that I thirst not, neither come hither to draw." Jesus saith unto her:—"Go, call thy husband, and come hither."

The woman answered and said:—"I have no husband." Jesus said unto her:—"Thou hast well said, I have no husband; for thou hast had five husbands; and he whom thou now hast is not thy husband: in that saidst thou truly."

The woman saith unto him:—"Sir, I perceive that thou art a prophet. Our fathers worshipped in this mountain; and ye say, that in Jerusalem is the place where men ought to worship." Jesus saith unto her:—"Woman, believe me, the hour cometh, when ye shall neither in this mountain, nor yet at Jerusalem, worship the Father. Ye worship ye know not what: we know what we worship: for salvation is of the Jews. But the hour cometh, and now is, when the true worshippers shall worship the Father in spirit and in truth: for the Father seeketh such to worship him. God is a spirit: and they that worship him must worship him in spirit and in truth."

The woman saith unto him :—"I know that Messiah cometh, which is called Christ: when he is come, he will tell us all things." Jesus saith unto her:—"I that speak unto thee am he."

ST JOHN IV (1–26)

[48]

PHILLIPPE DE CHAMPAIGNE (1602–74)   *Museum, Caen*

JESUS AND THE WOMAN OF SAMARIA

JESUS CALLS PETER, ANDREW, JAMES AND JOHN

AND he came down to Capernaum, a city of Galilee, and taught them on the sabbath days. And they were astonished at his doctrine: for his word was with power.

ST LUKE IV (31–32)

AND it came to pass, that, as the people pressed upon him to hear the word of God, he stood by the lake of Gennesaret, and saw two ships standing by the lake: but the fishermen were gone out of them, and were washing their nets. And he entered into one of the ships, which was Simon's, and prayed him that he would thrust out a little from the land. And he sat down, and taught the people out of the ship.

Now when he had left speaking, he said unto Simon:—"Launch out into the deep, and let down your nets for a draught." And Simon answering said unto him:—"Master, we have toiled all the night, and have taken nothing: nevertheless at thy word I will let down the net." And when they had this done, they inclosed a great multitude of fishes: and their net brake. And they beckoned unto their partners, which were in the other ship, that they should come and help them. And they came, and filled both the ships, so that they began to sink. When Simon Peter saw it, he fell down at Jesus' knees, saying:— "Depart from me; for I am a sinful man, O Lord." For he was astonished, and all that were with him, at the draught of the fishes which they had taken: and so was also James, and John, the sons of Zebedee, which were partners with Simon. And Jesus said unto Simon:—"Fear not; from henceforth thou shalt catch men." And when they had brought their ships to land, they forsook all, and followed him.

ST LUKE V (1–11)

RUBENS (1577–1640)   *Nôtre Dame au delà de la Dyle, Malines*

THE MIRACULOUS DRAUGHT OF FISHES

JESUS CURES A MAN WITH AN UNCLEAN SPIRIT

AND they went into Capernaum; and straightway on the sabbath day he entered into the synagogue, and taught. And they were astonished at his doctrine: for he taught them as one that had authority, and not as the scribes. And there was in their synagogue a man with an unclean spirit; and he cried out, saying:—"Let us alone; what have we to do with thee, thou Jesus of Nazareth? art thou come to destroy us? I know thee who thou art, the Holy One of God." And Jesus rebuked him, saying:—"Hold thy peace, and come out of him." And when the unclean spirit had torn him, and cried with a loud voice, he came out of him. And they were all amazed, insomuch that they questioned among themselves, saying:—"What thing is this? what new doctrine is this? for with authority commandeth he even the unclean spirits, and they do obey him." And immediately his fame spread abroad throughout all the region round about Galilee.

ST MARK I (21–28)

JESUS CURES PETER'S WIFE'S MOTHER AND OTHERS

AND forthwith, when they were come out of the synagogue, they entered into the house of Simon and Andrew, with James and John. But Simon's wife's mother lay sick of a fever, and anon they tell him of her. And he came and took her by the hand, and lifted her up; and immediately the fever left her, and she ministered unto them.

And at even, when the sun did set, they brought unto him all that were diseased, and them that were possessed with devils. And all the city was gathered together at the door. And he healed many that were sick of divers diseases, and cast out many devils; and suffered not the devils to speak, because they knew him.

ST MARK I (29–34)

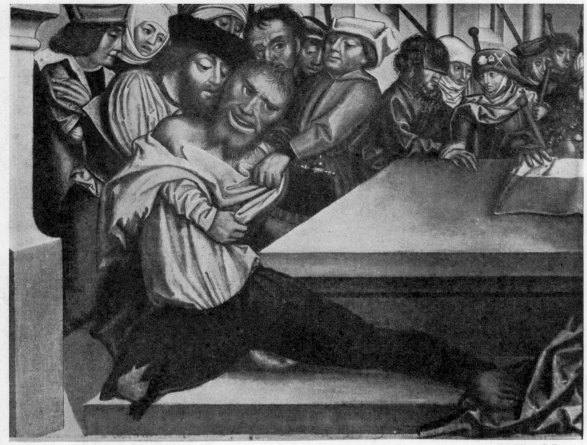

HANS FRIES (1460–1518)   (A detail from "The Tomb of St Anthony of Padua")   *Cordeliers, Fribourg*

THE MAN WITH AN UNCLEAN SPIRIT

FROM AN ARMENIAN MS. OF THE GOSPEL (XIII Century)
*Courtesy of the Freer Gallery of Art, Smithsonian Institution,
Washington, D.C.*

JESUS CURING PETER'S WIFE'S MOTHER

JESUS HEALS A LEPER

AND he preached in their synagogues throughout all Galilee, and cast out devils.

And there came a leper to him, beseeching him, and kneeling down to him, and saying unto him:—"If thou wilt, thou canst make me clean." And Jesus, moved with compassion, put forth His hand, and touched him, and saith unto him:—"I will; be thou clean." And as soon as he had spoken, immediately the leprosy departed from him, and he was cleansed. And he straitly charged him, and forthwith sent him away; and saith unto him:—"See thou say nothing to any man: but go thy way, shew thyself to the priest, and offer for thy cleansing those things which Moses commanded, for a testimony unto them." But he went out, and began to publish it much, and to blaze abroad the matter, insomuch that Jesus could no more openly enter into the city, but was without in desert places: and they came to him from every quarter.

ST MARK I (39–45)

JESUS HEALS A MAN SICK OF THE PALSY

AND again he entered into Capernaum after some days; and it was noised that he was in the house. And straightway many were gathered together, insomuch that there was no room to receive them, no, not so much as about the door: and he preached the word unto them. And they come unto him, bringing one sick of the palsy, which was borne of four. And when they could not come nigh unto him for the press, they uncovered the roof where he was: and when they had broken it up, they let down the bed wherein the sick of the palsy lay. When Jesus saw their faith, he said unto the sick of the palsy:—"Son, thy sins be forgiven thee." But there were certain of the scribes sitting there, and reasoning in their hearts, why doth this man thus speak blasphemies? who can forgive sins but God only? And immediately when Jesus perceived in his spirit that they so reasoned within themselves, he said unto them:—"Why reason ye these things in your hearts? Whether is it easier to say to the sick of the palsy, Thy sins be forgiven thee; or to say, Arise, and take up thy bed, and walk? But that ye may know that the Son of man hath power on earth to forgive sins, (he saith to the sick of the palsy,) I say unto thee, Arise, and take up thy bed, and go thy way into thine house." And immediately he arose, took up the bed, and went forth before them all; insomuch that they were all amazed, and glorified God, saying:—"We never saw it on this fashion."

ST MARK II (1–12)

**JESUS HEALING
A LEPER**

COSIMO ROSSELLI (1439–1507)   *Sistine Chapel, Rome*
(A detail from "The Sermon on the Mount")

**JESUS HEALING A MAN
SICK OF THE PALSY**

FROM A MORALISED BIBLE HISTORY
(French; end of XIII Century)
British Museum, London

AND as Jesus passed forth from thence, he saw a man, named Matthew, sitting at the receipt of custom: and he saith unto him:—"Follow me." And he arose, and followed him.

And it came to pass, as Jesus sat at meat in the house, behold, many publicans and sinners came and sat down with him and his disciples. And when the Pharisees saw it, they said unto his disciples:—"Why eateth your Master with publicans and sinners?" But when Jesus heard that, he said unto them:—"They that be whole need not a physician, but they that are sick. But go ye and learn what that meaneth, I will have mercy, and not sacrifice: for I am not come to call the righteous, but sinners to repentance."

Then came to him the disciples of John, saying:—"Why do we and the Pharisees fast oft, but thy disciples fast not?" And Jesus said unto them:—"Can the children of the bridechamber mourn, as long as the bridegroom is with them? but the days will come, when the bridegroom shall be taken from them, and then shall they fast. No man putteth a piece of new cloth unto an old garment, for that which is put in to fill it up taketh from the garment, and the rent is made worse. Neither do men put new wine into old bottles: else the bottles break, and the wine runneth out, and the bottles perish: but they put new wine into new bottles, and both are preserved."

ST MATTHEW IX (9–17)

ANTWERP SCHOOL (c. 1525)   *Windsor Castle (reproduced by gracious permission of H.M. the King)*

THE CALLING OF MATTHEW

THE CURE AT THE POOL OF BETHESDA

AFTER this there was a feast of the Jews; and Jesus went up to Jerusalem. Now there is at Jerusalem by the sheep market a pool, which is called in the Hebrew tongue Bethesda, having five porches. In these lay a great multitude of impotent folk, of blind, halt, withered, waiting for the moving of the water. For an angel went down at a certain season into the pool, and troubled the water: whosoever then first after the troubling of the water stepped in was made whole of whatsoever disease he had. And a certain man was there, which had an infirmity thirty and eight years. When Jesus saw him lie, and knew that he had been now a long time in that case, he saith unto him:— "Wilt thou be made whole?" The impotent man answered him:—"Sir, I have no man, when the water is troubled, to put me into the pool: but while I am coming, another steppeth down before me." Jesus saith unto him:—"Rise, take up thy bed, and walk." And immediately the man was made whole, and took up his bed, and walked: and on the same day was the sabbath. The Jews therefore said unto him that was cured:—"It is the sabbath day: it is not lawful for thee to carry thy bed." He answered them:—"He that made me whole, the same said unto me, Take up thy bed, and walk." Then asked they him:— "What man is that which said unto thee, Take up thy bed, and walk?" And he that was healed wist not who it was: for Jesus had conveyed himself away, a multitude being in that place. Afterward Jesus findeth him in the temple, and said unto him:—"Behold, thou art made whole: sin no more, lest a worse thing come unto thee." The man departed, and told the Jews that it was Jesus which had made him whole.

ST JOHN V (1–15)

VERONESE (1528–88)   *Museo Civico, Vicenza*

THE CURE AT THE POOL OF BETHESDA

JESUS TALKS ABOUT THE SABBATH

AND it came to pass, that he went through the cornfields on the sabbath day; and his disciples began, as they went, to pluck the ears of corn. And the Pharisees said unto him:—"Behold, why do they on the sabbath day that which is not lawful?" And he said unto them:—"Have ye never read what David did, when he had need, and was an hungered, he, and they that were with him? How he went into the house of God in the days of Abiathar the high priest, and did eat the shewbread, which is not lawful to eat but for the priests, and gave also to them which were with him?" And he said unto them: —"The sabbath was made for man, and not man for the sabbath: therefore the Son of man is Lord also of the sabbath."

ST MARK II (23–28)

JESUS HEALS THE MAN WITH A WITHERED HAND

AND he entered again into the synagogue; and there was a man there which had a withered hand. And they watched him, whether he would heal him on the sabbath day; that they might accuse him. And he saith unto the man which had the withered hand:—"Stand forth." And he saith unto them:— "Is it lawful to do good on the sabbath days, or to do evil? to save life, or to kill?" But they held their peace. And when he had looked round about on them with anger, being grieved for the hardness of their hearts, he saith unto the man:—"Stretch forth thine hand." And he stretched it out: and his hand was restored whole as the other. And the Pharisees went forth, and straightway took counsel with the Herodians against him, how they might destroy him.

ST MARK III (1–6)

JESUS CHOOSES THE TWELVE APOSTLES

AND he goeth up into a mountain, and calleth unto him whom he would: and they came unto him. And he ordained twelve, that they should be with him, and that he might send them forth to preach, and to have power to heal sicknesses, and to cast out devils: and Simon he surnamed Peter; and James the son of Zebedee, and John the brother of James; and he surnamed them Boanerges, which is the sons of thunder: and Andrew, and Philip, and Bartholomew, and Matthew, and Thomas, and James the son of Alphæus, and Thaddæus and Simon the Canaanite, and Judas Iscariot, which also betrayed him.

ST MARK III (13–19)

JESUS AND HIS DISCIPLES PLUCKING CORN

FROM A MORALISED BIBLE HISTORY
(French; end of XIII Century)
British Museum, London

JESUS HEALING THE MAN WITH THE WITHERED HAND

ROM AN ARMENIAN MS. OF THE GOSPEL (XIII Century)
*Courtesy of the Freer Gallery of Art, Smithsonian Institution,
Washington, D.C.*

JESUS WITH THE TWELVE APOSTLES

FROM AN ARMENIAN MS. OF THE GOSPEL
(XIII Century)
*Courtesy of the Freer Gallery of Art, Smithsonian Institution,
Washington, D.C.*

AND seeing the multitudes, he went up into a mountain: and when he was set, his disciples came unto him: and he opened his mouth, and taught them, saying:—"Blessed are the poor in spirit: for theirs is the kingdom of heaven. Blessed are they that mourn: for they shall be comforted. Blessed are the meek: for they shall inherit the earth. Blessed are they which do hunger and thirst after righteousness: for they shall be filled. Blessed are the merciful: for they shall obtain mercy. Blessed are the pure in heart: for they shall see God. Blessed are the peacemakers: for they shall be called the children of God. Blessed are they which are persecuted for righteousness' sake: for theirs is the kingdom of heaven. Blessed are ye, when men shall revile you, and persecute you, and shall say all manner of evil against you falsely, for my sake. Rejoice, and be exceeding glad: for great is your reward in heaven: for so persecuted they the prophets which were before you. Ye are the salt of the earth: but if the salt have lost his savour, wherewith shall it be salted? it is thenceforth good for nothing, but to be cast out, and to be trodden under foot of men."

ST MATTHEW V (1–13)

QUINTIN MATSYS (c. 1466–1530)   *Kunstmuseum, Winterthur*

JESUS BLESSING

"YE are the light of the world. A city that is set on an hill cannot be hid. Neither do men light a candle, and put it under a bushel, but on a candle-stick; and it giveth light unto all that are in the house. Let your light so shine before men, that they may see your good works, and glorify your Father which is in heaven.

"Think not that I am come to destroy the law, or the prophets: I am not come to destroy, but to fulfil. For verily I say unto you, Till heaven and earth pass, one jot or one tittle shall in no wise pass from the law, till all be fulfilled. Whosoever therefore shall break one of these least commandments, and shall teach men so, he shall be called the least in the kingdom of heaven: but whosoever shall do and teach them, the same shall be called great in the kingdom of heaven. For I say unto you, that except your righteousness shall exceed the righteousness of the scribes and Pharisees, ye shall in no case enter into the kingdom of heaven.

"Ye have heard that it was said by them of old time, Thou shalt not kill; and whosoever shall kill shall be in danger of the judgment: but I say unto you, that whosoever is angry with his brother without a cause shall be in danger of the judgment: and whosoever shall say to his brother, Raca, shall be in danger of the council: but whosoever shall say, Thou fool, shall be in danger of hell fire. Therefore if thou bring thy gift to the altar, and there rememberest that thy brother hath ought against thee; leave there thy gift before the altar, and go thy way; first be reconciled to thy brother, and then come and offer thy gift. Agree with thine adversary quickly, whiles thou art in the way with him; lest at any time the adversary deliver thee to the judge, and the judge deliver thee to the officer, and thou be cast into prison. Verily I say unto thee, Thou shalt by no means come out thence, till thou hast paid the uttermost farthing.

"Ye have heard that it was said by them of old time, Thou shalt not commit adultery: but I say unto you, that whosoever looketh on a woman to lust after her hath committed adultery with her already in his heart. And if thy right eye offend thee, pluck it out, and cast it from thee: for it is profitable for thee that one of thy members should perish, and not that thy whole body should be cast into hell. And if thy right hand offend thee, cut it off, and cast it from thee: for it is profitable for thee that one of thy members should perish, and not that thy whole body should be cast into hell.

MANTEGNA (1431–1506)   *Musée des Beaux-Arts, Tours*

(A detail from "Christ in the Garden of Olives")

A CITY SET ON A HILL

"IT hath been said, Whosoever shall put away his wife, let him give her a writing of divorcement: but I say unto you, that whosoever shall put away his wife, saving for the cause of fornication, causeth her to commit adultery: and whosoever shall marry her that is divorced committeth adultery.

"Again, ye have heard that it hath been said by them of old time, Thou shalt not forswear thyself, but shalt perform unto the Lord thine oaths: but I say unto you, Swear not at all; neither by heaven; for it is God's throne: nor by the earth; for it is his footstool: neither by Jerusalem; for it is the city of the great King. Neither shalt thou swear by thy head, because thou canst not make one hair white or black. But let your communication be, Yea, yea; Nay, nay: for whatsoever is more than these cometh of evil.

"Ye have heard that it hath been said, An eye for an eye, and a tooth for a tooth: but I say unto you, that ye resist not evil: but whosoever shall smite thee on thy right cheek, turn to him the other also. And if any man will sue thee at the law, and take away thy coat, let him have thy cloke also. And whosoever shall compel thee to go a mile, go with him twain. Give to him that asketh thee, and from him that would borrow of thee turn not thou away.

"Ye have heard that it hath been said, Thou shalt love thy neighbour, and hate thine enemy. But I say unto you, Love your enemies, bless them that curse you, do good to them that hate you, and pray for them which despitefully use you, and persecute you; that ye may be the children of your Father which is in heaven: for he maketh his sun to rise on the evil and on the good, and sendeth rain on the just and on the unjust. For if ye love them which love you, what reward have ye? do not even the publicans the same? And if ye salute your brethren only, what do ye more than others? do not even the publicans so? Be ye therefore perfect, even as your Father which is in heaven is perfect.

"Take heed that ye do not your alms before men, to be seen of them: otherwise ye have no reward of your Father which is in heaven. Therefore when thou doest thine alms, do not sound a trumpet before thee, as the hypocrites do in the synagogues and in the streets, that they may have glory of men. Verily I say unto you, They have their reward. But when thou doest alms, let not thy left hand know what thy right hand doeth: that thine alms may be in secret: and thy Father which seeth in secret himself shall reward thee openly.

COSIMO ROSSELLI (1439–1507)   *Sistine Chapel, Rome*

THE SERMON ON THE MOUNT

"AND when thou prayest, thou shalt not be as the hypocrites are: for they love to pray standing in the synagogues and in the corners of the streets, that they may be seen of men. Verily I say unto you, They have their reward. But thou, when thou prayest, enter into thy closet, and when thou hast shut thy door, pray to thy Father which is in secret; and thy Father which seeth in secret shall reward thee openly. But when ye pray, use not vain repetitions, as the heathen do: for they think that they shall be heard for their much speaking. Be not ye therefore like unto them: for your Father knoweth what things ye have need of, before ye ask him. After this manner therefore pray ye:— Our Father which art in heaven, Hallowed be thy name. Thy kingdom come. Thy will be done in earth, as it is in heaven. Give us this day our daily bread. And forgive us our debts, as we forgive our debtors. And lead us not into temptation, but deliver us from evil: for Thine is the kingdom, and the power, and the glory, for ever. Amen. For if ye forgive men their trespasses, your heavenly Father will also forgive you: but if ye forgive not men their trespasses, neither will your Father forgive your trespasses.

"Moreover when ye fast, be not, as the hypocrites, of a sad countenance: for they disfigure their faces, that they may appear unto men to fast. Verily I say unto you, they have their reward. But thou, when thou fastest, anoint thine head, and wash thy face; that thou appear not unto men to fast, but unto thy Father which is in secret: and thy Father, which seeth in secret, shall reward thee openly.

"Lay not up for yourselves treasures upon earth, where moth and rust doth corrupt, and where thieves break through and steal: but lay up for yourselves treasures in heaven, where neither moth nor rust doth corrupt, and where thieves do not break through nor steal: for where your treasure is, there will your heart be also. The light of the body is the eye: if therefore thine eye be single, thy whole body shall be full of light. But if thine eye be evil, thy whole body shall be full of darkness. If therefore the light that is in thee be darkness, how great is that darkness!

"No man can serve two masters: for either he will hate the one, and love the other; or else he will hold to the one, and despise the other. Ye cannot serve God and mammon. Therefore I say unto you, Take no thought for your life, what ye shall eat, or what ye shall drink; nor yet for your body, what ye shall put on. Is not the life more than meat, and the body than raiment?

DÜRER (1471–1528)   *Albertina, Vienna*

("Praying Hands")

OUR FATHER WHICH ART IN HEAVEN . . .

"BEHOLD the fowls of the air: for they sow not, neither do they reap, nor gather into barns; yet your heavenly Father feedeth them. Are ye not much better than they? Which of you by taking thought can add one cubit unto his stature? And why take ye thought for raiment? Consider the lilies of the field, how they grow; they toil not, neither do they spin: and yet I say unto you, that even Solomon in all his glory was not arrayed like one of these. Wherefore if God so clothe the grass of the field, which to day is, and to morrow is cast into the oven, shall he not much more clothe you, O ye of little faith? Therefore take no thought, saying, What shall we eat? or, What shall we drink? or, Wherewithal shall we be clothed? (For after all these things do the Gentiles seek:) for your heavenly Father knoweth that ye have need of all these things. But seek ye first the kingdom of God, and his righteousness; and all these things shall be added unto you. Take therefore no thought for the morrow: for the morrow shall take thought for the things of itself. Sufficient unto the day is the evil thereof.

"Judge not, that ye be not judged. For with what judgment ye judge, ye shall be judged: and with what measure ye mete, it shall be measured to you again. And why beholdest thou the mote that is in thy brother's eye, but considerest not the beam that is in thine own eye? Or how wilt thou say to thy brother, Let me pull out the mote out of thine eye; and, behold, a beam is in thine own eye? Thou hypocrite, first cast out the beam out of thine own eye; and then shalt thou see clearly to cast out the mote out of thy brother's eye. Give not that which is holy unto the dogs, neither cast ye your pearls before swine, lest they trample them under their feet, and turn again and rend you.

"Ask, and it shall be given you; seek, and ye shall find; knock, and it shall be opened unto you. For every one that asketh receiveth; and he that seeketh findeth; and to him that knocketh it shall be opened. Or what man is there of you, whom if his son ask bread, will he give him a stone? Or if he ask a fish, will he give him a serpent? If ye then, being evil, know how to give good gifts unto your children, how much more shall your Father which is in heaven give good things to them that ask him? Therefore all things whatsoever ye would that men should do to you, do ye even so to them: for this is the law and the prophets.

[70]

DOMENICO FETI (c. 1589–1624)

Collection of F. D. Lycett Green, Esq.

THE PARABLE OF THE MOTE AND THE BEAM

"'ENTER ye in at the strait gate: for wide is the gate, and broad is the way, that leadeth to destruction, and many there be which go in thereat: because strait is the gate, and narrow is the way, which leadeth unto life, and few there be that find it.

"Beware of false prophets, which come to you in sheep's clothing, but inwardly they are ravening wolves. Ye shall know them by their fruits. Do men gather grapes of thorns, or figs of thistles? Even so every good tree bringeth forth good fruit; but a corrupt tree bringeth forth evil fruit. A good tree cannot bring forth evil fruit, neither can a corrupt tree bring forth good fruit. Every tree that bringeth not forth good fruit is hewn down, and cast into the fire. Wherefore by their fruits ye shall know them. Not every one that saith unto me, Lord, Lord, shall enter into the kingdom of heaven; but he that doeth the will of my Father which is in heaven. Many will say to me in that day, Lord, Lord, have we not prophesied in thy name? and in thy name have cast out devils? and in thy name done many wonderful works? And then will I profess unto them, I never knew you: depart from me, ye that work iniquity.

"Therefore whosoever heareth these sayings of mine, and doeth them, I will liken him unto a wise man, which built his house upon a rock: and the rain descended, and the floods came, and the winds blew, and beat upon that house; and it fell not: for it was founded upon a rock. And every one that heareth these sayings of mine, and doeth them not, shall be likened unto a foolish man, which built his house upon the sand: and the rain descended, and the floods came, and the winds blew, and beat upon that house; and it fell: and great was the fall of it."

And it came to pass, when Jesus had ended these sayings, the people were astonished at his doctrine: for he taught them as one having authority, and not as the scribes.

ST MATTHEW V (14–48), VI, VII

GIOVANNI BELLINI (1431?–1516)   National Gallery, London

(A detail from "Madonna and Child")

THE HOUSE BUILT UPON A ROCK

JESUS HEALS THE CENTURION'S SERVANT

WHEN he was come down from the mountain, great multitudes followed him. And when Jesus was entered into Capernaum, there came unto him a centurion, beseeching him, and saying:—"Lord, my servant lieth at home sick of the palsy, grievously tormented." And Jesus saith unto him:—"I will come and heal him." The centurion answered and said:—"Lord, I am not worthy that thou shouldest come under my roof: but speak the word only, and my servant shall be healed. For I am a man under authority, having soldiers under me: and I say to this man, Go, and he goeth; and to another, Come, and he cometh; and to my servant, Do this, and he doeth it." When Jesus heard it, he marvelled, and said to them that followed:—"Verily I say unto you, I have not found so great faith, no, not in Israel. And I say unto you, that many shall come from the east and west, and shall sit down with Abraham, and Isaac, and Jacob, in the kingdom of heaven. But the children of the kingdom shall be cast out into outer darkness: there shall be weeping and gnashing of teeth." And Jesus said unto the centurion:—"Go thy way; and as thou hast believed, so be it done unto thee." And his servant was healed in the selfsame hour.

ST MATTHEW VIII (1, 5-13)

JESUS RAISES FROM THE DEAD THE WIDOW'S SON

AND it came to pass the day after, that he went into a city called Nain; and many of his disciples went with him, and much people. Now when he came nigh to the gate of the city, behold, there was a dead man carried out, the only son of his mother, and she was a widow: and much people of the city was with her. And when the Lord saw her, he had compassion on her, and said unto her:—"Weep not." And he came and touched the bier: and they that bare him stood still. And he said:—"Young man, I say unto thee, Arise." And he that was dead sat up, and began to speak. And he delivered him to his mother. And there came a fear on all: and they glorified God, saying, that a great prophet is risen up among us; and, that God hath visited his people. And this rumour of him went forth throughout all Judæa, and throughout all the region round about.

ST LUKE VII (11-17)

VERONESE (1528–88)   Prado, Madrid

JESUS AND THE CENTURION

FROM THE CODEX AUREUS   Monastery of San Lorenzo el Real,
(German; c. 1045)   Escorial, Madrid

THE RESURRECTION OF THE WIDOW'S SON

THE WOMAN ANOINTS JESUS' FEET

AND one of the Pharisees desired him that he would eat with him. And he went into the Pharisee's house, and sat down to meat. And, behold, a woman in the city, which was a sinner, when she knew that Jesus sat at meat in the Pharisee's house, brought an alabaster box of ointment, and stood at his feet behind him weeping, and began to wash his feet with tears, and did wipe them with the hairs of her head, and kissed his feet, and anointed them with the ointment. Now when the Pharisee which had bidden him saw it, he spake within himself, saying, This man, if he were a prophet, would have known who and what manner of woman this is that toucheth him: for she is a sinner. And Jesus answering said unto him:—"Simon, I have somewhat to say unto thee." And he saith:—"Master, say on." "There was a certain creditor which had two debtors: the one owed five hundred pence, and the other fifty. And when they had nothing to pay, he frankly forgave them both. Tell me therefore, which of them will love him most?"

Simon answered and said:—"I suppose that he, to whom he forgave most." And he said unto him:—"Thou hast rightly judged." And he turned to the woman, and said unto Simon:—"Seest thou this woman? I entered into thine house, thou gavest me no water for my feet: but she hath washed my feet with tears, and wiped them with the hairs of her head. Thou gavest me no kiss: but this woman since the time I came in hath not ceased to kiss my feet. My head with oil thou didst not anoint: but this woman hath anointed my feet with ointment. Wherefore I say unto thee, her sins, which are many, are forgiven; for she loved much: but to whom little is forgiven, the same loveth little." And he said unto her:—"Thy sins are forgiven." And they that sat at meat with him began to say within themselves, "Who is this that forgiveth sins also?" And he said to the woman:—"Thy faith hath saved thee; go in peace."

ST LUKE VII (36–50)

JESUS HEALS MARY MAGDALENE, AND OTHERS

AND it came to pass afterward, that he went throughout every city and village, preaching and shewing the glad tidings of the kingdom of God: and the twelve were with him, and certain women, which had been healed of evil spirits and infirmities, Mary called Magdalene, out of whom went seven devils, and Joanna the wife of Chuza, Herod's steward, and Susanna, and many others, which ministered unto him of their substance.

ST LUKE VIII (1–3)

VERONESE (1528–88)

Reale Pinacoteca, Turin

("The Supper in the House of Simon the Pharisee")

THE WOMAN ANOINTING JESUS' FEET

AND he began again to teach by the sea side: and there was gathered unto him a great multitude, so that he entered into a ship, and sat in the sea: and the whole multitude was by the sea on the land. And he taught them many things by parables, and said unto them in his doctrine:—"Hearken; Behold there went out a sower to sow: and it came to pass, as he sowed, some fell by the way side, and the fowls of the air came and devoured it up. And some fell on stony ground, where it had not much earth; and immediately it sprang up, because it had no depth of earth: but when the sun was up, it was scorched; and because it had no root, it withered away. And some fell among thorns, and the thorns grew up, and choked it, and it yielded no fruit. And other fell on good ground, and did yield fruit that sprang up and increased; and brought forth, some thirty, and some sixty, and some an hundred." And he said unto them:—"He that hath ears to hear, let him hear." And when he was alone, they that were about him with the twelve asked of him the parable. And he said unto them:—"Unto you it is given to know the mystery of the kingdom of God; but unto them that are without all these things are done in parables: that seeing they may see, and not perceive; and hearing they may hear, and not understand; lest at any time they should be converted, and their sins should be forgiven them."

And he said unto them:—"Know ye not this parable? and how then will ye know all parables? The sower soweth the word. And these are they by the way side, where the word is sown; but when they have heard, Satan cometh immediately, and taketh away the word that was sown in their hearts. And these are they likewise which are sown on stony ground; who, when they have heard the word, immediately receive it with gladness; and have no root in themselves, and so endure but for a time: afterward, when affliction or persecution ariseth for the word's sake, immediately they are offended. And these are they which are sown among thorns; such as hear the word, and the cares of this world, and the deceitfulness of riches, and the lusts of other things entering in, choke the word, and it becometh unfruitful. And these are they which are sown on good ground; such as hear the word, and receive it, and bring forth fruit, some thirtyfold, some sixty, and some an hundred."

ST MARK IV (1–20)

[78]

POL DE LIMBOURG (Born *c.* 1380) AND HIS BROTHERS   *Musé Condé, Chantilly*
("October: Sowing")

THE SOWER

ANOTHER parable put he forth unto them, saying:—"The kingdom of heaven is likened unto a man which sowed good seed in his field: but while men slept, his enemy came and sowed tares among the wheat, and went his way. But when the blade was sprung up, and brought forth fruit, then appeared the tares also. So the servants of the householder came and said unto him, Sir, didst not thou sow good seed in thy field? from whence then hath it tares? He said unto them, An enemy hath done this. The servants said unto him, Wilt thou then that we go and gather them up? But he said, Nay; lest while ye gather up the tares, ye root up also the wheat with them. Let both grow together until the harvest: and in the time of harvest I will say to the reapers, gather ye together first the tares, and bind them in bundles to burn them: but gather the wheat into my barn."

Another parable put he forth unto them, saying:—"The kingdom of heaven is like to a grain of mustard seed, which a man took, and sowed in his field: which indeed is the least of all seeds: but when it is grown, it is the greatest among herbs, and becometh a tree, so that the birds of the air come and lodge in the branches thereof."

Another parable spake he unto them:—"The kingdom of heaven is like unto leaven, which a woman took, and hid in three measures of meal, till the whole was leavened."

All these things spake Jesus unto the multitude in parables; and without a parable spake he not unto them: that it might be fulfilled which was spoken by the prophet, saying:—I will open my mouth in parables; I will utter things which have been kept secret from the foundation of the world.

Then Jesus sent the multitude away, and went into the house: and his disciples come unto him, saying:—"Declare unto us the parable of the tares of the field." He answered and said unto them:—"He that soweth the good seed is the Son of man: the field is the world; the good seed are the children of the kingdom; but the tares are the children of the wicked one; the enemy that sowed them is the devil; the harvest is the end of the world; and the reapers are the angels. As therefore the tares are gathered and burned in the fire; so shall it be in the end of this world. The Son of man shall send forth his angels, and they shall gather out of his kingdom all things that offend, and them which do iniquity; and shall cast them into a furnace of fire: there shall be wailing and gnashing of teeth. Then shall the righteous shine forth as the sun in the kingdom of their Father. Who hath ears to hear, let him hear."

ST MATTHEW XIII (24–43)

DOMENICO FETI (c. 1589–1624)

THE ENEMY SOWING TARES

JESUS STILLS THE TEMPEST

NOW it came to pass on a certain day, that he went into a ship with his disciples: and he said unto them:—"Let us go over unto the other side of the lake." And they launched forth. But as they sailed he fell asleep: and there came down a storm of wind on the lake; and they were filled with water, and were in jeopardy. And they came to him, and awoke him, saying:—"Master, Master, we perish." Then he arose, and rebuked the wind and the raging of the water: and they ceased, and there was a calm. And he said unto them:— "Where is your faith?" And they being afraid wondered, saying one to another, "What manner of man is this! for he commandeth even the winds and water, and they obey him."

ST LUKE VIII (22–25)

JESUS HEALS A LUNATIC

AND they arrived at the country of the Gadarenes, which is over against Galilee. And when he went forth to land, there met him out of the city a certain man, which had devils long time, and ware no clothes, neither abode in any house, but in the tombs. When he saw Jesus, he cried out and fell down before him, and with a loud voice said:—"What have I to do with thee, Jesus thou son of God most high? I beseech thee, torment me not." (For he had commanded the unclean spirit to come out of the man. For oftentimes it had caught him: and he was kept bound with chains and in fetters; and he brake the bands, and was driven of the devil into the wilderness.) And Jesus asked him saying:—"What is thy name?" And he said:—"Legion": because many devils were entered into him. And they besought him that he would not command them to go out into the deep. And there was there an herd of many swine feeding on the mountain: and they besought him that he would suffer them to enter into them. And he suffered them. Then went the devils out of the man, and entered into the swine: and the herd ran violently down a steep place into the lake, and were choked. When they that fed them saw what was done, they fled, and went and told it in the city and in the country. Then they went out to see what was done; and came to Jesus, and found the man, out of whom the devils were departed, sitting at the feet of Jesus, clothed and in his right mind: and they were afraid. They also which saw it told them by what means he that was possessed of the devils was healed. Then the whole multitude of the country of the Gadarenes round about besought him to depart from them; for they were taken with great fear: and he went up into the ship, and returned back again. Now the man out of whom the devils were departed besought him that he might be with him: but Jesus sent him away, saying:—"Return to thine own house, and shew how great things God hath done unto thee." And he went his way, and published throughout the whole city how great things Jesus had done unto him.

ST LUKE VIII (26–39)

[82]

THE STORM ON THE SEA OF GALILEE

JESUS HEALS THE WOMAN WITH AN ISSUE OF BLOOD
AND RAISES JAIRUS' DAUGHTER

AND when Jesus was passed over again by ship unto the other side, much people gathered unto him: and he was nigh unto the sea. And, behold, there cometh one of the rulers of the synagogue, Jairus by name; and when he saw him, he fell at his feet, and besought him greatly, saying:—"My little daughter lieth at the point of death: I pray thee come and lay thy hands on her, that she may be healed; and she shall live." And Jesus went with him; and much people followed him, and thronged him.

And a certain woman, which had an issue of blood twelve years, and had suffered many things of many physicians, and had spent all that she had, and was nothing bettered, but rather grew worse, when she had heard of Jesus, came in the press behind, and touched his garment. For she said, "If I may touch but his clothes, I shall be whole." And straightway the fountain of her blood was dried up; and she felt in her body that she was healed of that plague. And Jesus, immediately knowing in himself that virtue had gone out of him, turned him about in the press, and said:—"Who touched my clothes?" And his disciples said unto him:—"Thou seest the multitude thronging thee, and sayest thou, Who touched me?" And he looked round about to see her that had done this thing. But the woman fearing and trembling, knowing what was done in her, came and fell down before him, and told him all the truth. And he said unto her:—"Daughter, thy faith hath made thee whole; go in peace, and be whole of thy plague." While he yet spake, there came from the ruler of the synagogue's house certain which said:—"Thy daughter is dead: why troublest thou the Master any further?" As soon as Jesus heard the word that was spoken, he saith unto the ruler of the synagogue:—"Be not afraid, only believe." And he suffered no man to follow him, save Peter, and James, and John the brother of James. And he cometh to the house of the ruler of the synagogue, and seeth the tumult, and them that wept and wailed greatly. And when he was come in, he saith unto them:—"Why make ye this ado, and weep? the damsel is not dead, but sleepeth." And they laughed him to scorn. But when he had put them all out, he taketh the father and the mother of the damsel, and them that were with him, and entereth in where the damsel was lying. And he took the damsel by the hand, and said unto her, "Talitha cumi"; which is, being interpreted:—"Damsel, I say unto thee, arise." And straightway the damsel arose, and walked; for she was of the age of twelve years. And they were astonished with a great astonishment. And he charged them straitly that no man should know it; and commanded that something should be given her to eat.

ST MARK V (21-43)

[84]

SEBASTIANO RICCI (1659–1734)
MARCO RICCI (1676–1729)

Hampton Court Palace (reproduced by gracious permission of H.M. the King)

("Christ and the Woman who Believed")

DAUGHTER, THY FAITH HATH MADE THEE WHOLE

AND when he had called unto him his twelve disciples, he gave them power against unclean spirits, to cast them out, and to heal all manner of sickness and all manner of disease.

These twelve Jesus sent forth, and commanded them, saying:—"Go not into the way of the Gentiles, and into any city of the Samaritans enter ye not: but go rather to the lost sheep of the house of Israel. And as ye go, preach, saying:—The kingdom of heaven is at hand. Heal the sick, cleanse the lepers, raise the dead, cast out devils: freely ye have received, freely give. Provide neither gold, nor silver, nor brass in your purses, nor scrip for your journey, neither two coats, neither shoes, nor yet staves: for the workman is worthy of his meat. And into whatsoever city or town ye shall enter, inquire who in it is worthy; and there abide till ye go thence. And when ye come into an house, salute it. And if the house be worthy, let your peace come upon it: but if it be not worthy, let your peace return to you. And whosoever shall not receive you, nor hear your words, when ye depart out of that house or city, shake off the dust of your feet. Verily I say unto you, it shall be more tolerable for the land of Sodom and Gomorrha in the day of judgment, than for that city. Behold, I send you forth as sheep in the midst of wolves: be ye therefore wise as serpents, and harmless as doves. But beware of men: for they will deliver you up to the councils, and they will scourge you in their synagogues; and ye shall be brought before governors and kings for my sake, for a testimony against them and the Gentiles. But when they deliver you up, take no thought how or what ye shall speak: for it shall be given you in that same hour what ye shall speak. For it is not ye that speak, but the Spirit of your Father which speaketh in you."

ST MATTHEW X (I, 5–20)

MANTEGNA (1431–1506)   ("James the Greater before the Emperor")   *Eremitani, Padua*

YE SHALL BE BROUGHT BEFORE GOVERNORS AND KINGS FOR MY SAKE

JOHN THE BAPTIST IS BEHEADED

A N D king Herod heard of him: (for his name was spread abroad:) and he said, that John the Baptist was risen from the dead, and therefore mighty works do shew forth themselves in him. Others said, that it is Elijah. And others said, that it is a prophet, or as one of the prophets. But when Herod heard thereof, he said:—"It is John, whom I beheaded: he is risen from the dead." For Herod himself had sent forth and laid hold upon John, and bound him in prison for Herodias' sake, his brother Philip's wife: for he had married her. For John had said unto Herod, It is not lawful for thee to have thy brother's wife. Therefore Herodias had a quarrel against him, and would have killed him; but she could not: for Herod feared John, knowing that he was a just man and an holy, and observed him; and when he heard him, he did many things, and heard him gladly. And when a convenient day was come, that Herod on his birthday made a supper to his lords, high captains, and chief estates of Galilee; and when the daughter of the said Herodias came in, and danced, and pleased Herod and them that sat with him, the king said unto the damsel:—"Ask of me whatsoever thou wilt, and I will give it thee." And he sware unto her:—"Whatsoever thou shalt ask of me, I will give it thee, unto the half of my kingdom." And she went forth, and said unto her mother: —"What shall I ask?" And she said:—"The head of John the Baptist." And she came in straightway with haste unto the king, and asked, saying:—"I will that thou give me by and by in a charger the head of John the Baptist." And the king was exceeding sorry; yet for his oath's sake, and for their sakes which sat with him, he would not reject her. And immediately the king sent an executioner, and commanded his head to be brought: and he went and beheaded him in the prison and brought his head in a charger, and gave it to the damsel: and the damsel gave it to her mother. And when his disciples heard of it, they came and took up his corpse, and laid it in a tomb.

ST MARK VI (14–29)

LUCAS CRANACH (1472–1533) ("The Feast of Herod") *Courtesy of the Wadsworth Atheneum, Hartford, Connecticut*

SALOME WITH THE BAPTIST'S HEAD

WHEN Jesus heard of it, he departed thence by ship into a desert place apart: and when the people had heard thereof, they followed him on foot out of the cities. And Jesus went forth, and saw a great multitude, and was moved with compassion toward them, and he healed their sick. And when it was evening, his disciples came to him, saying:—"This is a desert place, and the time is now past; send the multitude away, that they may go into the villages, and buy themselves victuals." But Jesus said unto them:—"They need not depart; give ye them to eat." And they say unto him:—"We have here but five loaves, and two fishes." He said:—"Bring them hither to me." And he commanded the multitude to sit down on the grass, and took the five loaves, and the two fishes, and looking up to heaven, he blessed, and brake, and gave the loaves to his disciples, and the disciples to the multitude. And they did all eat, and were filled: and they took up of the fragments that remained twelve baskets full. And they that had eaten were about five thousand men, beside women and children.

And straightway Jesus constrained his disciples to get into a ship, and to go before him unto the other side, while he sent the multitudes away. And when he had sent the multitudes away, he went up into a mountain apart to pray: and when the evening was come, he was there alone. But the ship was now in the midst of the sea, tossed with waves: for the wind was contrary. And in the fourth watch of the night Jesus went unto them, walking on the sea. And when the disciples saw him walking on the sea, they were troubled, saying, it is a spirit; and they cried out for fear. But straightway Jesus spake unto them, saying:—"Be of good cheer; it is I; be not afraid." And Peter answered him and said:—"Lord, if it be thou, bid me come unto thee on the water." And he said:—"Come." And when Peter was come down out of the ship, he walked on the water, to go to Jesus. But when he saw the wind boisterous, he was afraid; and beginning to sink, he cried, saying:—"Lord, save me." And immediately Jesus stretched forth his hand, and caught him, and said unto him:—"O thou of little faith, wherefore didst thou doubt?" And when they were come into the ship, the wind ceased. Then they that were in the ship came and worshipped him, saying:—"Of a truth Thou art the Son of God."

And when they were gone over, they came into the land of Gennesaret.

ST MATTHEW XIV (13–34)

MURILLO (1618–82)   Ospedale della Carita, Seville

("The Miracle of the Loaves and Fishes")

THE FEEDING OF THE FIVE THOUSAND

FROM THE HUNTERIAN PSALTER (c. 1170)   Courtesy of Glasgow University

CHRIST SAVING PETER

THEN came to Jesus scribes and Pharisees, which were of Jerusalem, saying:—"Why do thy disciples transgress the tradition of the elders? for they wash not their hands when they eat bread." But he answered and said unto them:—"Why do ye also transgress the commandment of God by your tradition? For God commanded, saying:—Honour thy father and mother: and, He that curseth father or mother, let him die the death. But ye say, Whosoever shall say to his father or his mother, it is a gift, by whatsoever thou mightest be profited by me; and honour not his father or his mother, he shall be free. Thus have ye made the commandment of God of none effect by your tradition. Ye hypocrites, well did Isaiah prophesy of you, saying:—This people draweth nigh unto me with their mouth, And honoureth me with their lips; But their heart is far from me. But in vain they do worship me, Teaching for doctrines the commandments of men." And he called the multitude, and said unto them:—"Hear, and understand. Not that which goeth into the mouth defileth a man; but that which cometh out of the mouth, this defileth a man."

Then came his disciples, and said unto him:—"Knowest thou that the Pharisees were offended, after they heard this saying?" But he answered and said:—"Every plant, which my heavenly Father hath not planted, shall be rooted up. Let them alone: they be blind leaders of the blind. And if the blind lead the blind, both shall fall into the ditch."

ST MATTHEW XV (1–14)

JESUS HEALS THE DAUGHTER OF THE SYROPHENICIAN WOMAN

AND from thence he arose, and went into the borders of Tyre and Sidon, and entered into an house, and would have no man know it: but he could not be hid. For a certain woman, whose young daughters had an unclean spirit, heard of him, and came and fell at his feet. The woman was a Greek, a Syrophenician by nation; and she besought him that he would cast forth the devil out of her daughter. But Jesus said unto her:—"Let the children first be filled: for it is not meet to take the children's bread, and to cast it unto the dogs." And she answered and said unto him:—"Yes, Lord: yet the dogs under the table eat of the children's crumbs." And he said unto her:—"For this saying go thy way: the devil is gone out of thy daughter." And when she was come to her house, she found the devil gone out, and her daughter laid upon the bed.

ST MARK VII (24–30)

P. BREUGHEL THE ELDER (c. 1525–70) *Museo Nazionale, Naples*

THE BLIND LEADING THE BLIND

JESUS HEALING THE DAUGHTER
OF THE SYROPHENICIAN WOMAN

FROM A MORALISED BIBLE HISTORY
(French; end of XIII Century) *British Museum, London*

THE FEEDING OF THE FOUR THOUSAND

THEN Jesus called his disciples unto him, and said:—"I have compassion on the multitude, because they continue with me now three days, and have nothing to eat: and I will not send them away fasting, lest they faint in the way." And his disciples say unto him:—"Whence should we have so much bread in the wilderness, as to fill so great a multitude?" And Jesus saith unto them:—"How many loaves have ye?" And they said:—"Seven, and a few little fishes." And he commanded the multitude to sit down on the ground. And he took the seven loaves and the fishes, and gave thanks, and brake them, and gave to his disciples, and the disciples to the multitude. And they did all eat, and were filled: and they took up of the broken meat that was left seven baskets full. And they that did eat were four thousand men, beside women and children. And he sent away the multitude, and took ship, and came into the coasts of Magdala.

ST MATTHEW XV (32–39)

THE LEAVEN OF PHARISEES

AND when his disciples were come to the other side, they had forgotten to take bread. Then Jesus said unto them:—"Take heed and beware of the leaven of the Pharisees and of the Sadducees." And they reasoned among themselves, saying:—"It is because we have taken no bread." Which when Jesus perceived, he said unto them:—"O ye of little faith, why reason ye among yourselves, because ye have brought no bread? Do ye not yet understand, neither remember the five loaves of the five thousand, and how many baskets ye took up? Neither the seven loaves of the four thousand, and how many baskets ye took up? How is it that ye do not understand that I spake it not to you concerning bread, that ye should beware of the leaven of the Pharisees and of the Sadducees?" Then understood they how that he bade them not beware of the leaven of bread, but of the doctrine of the Pharisees and of the Sadducees.

ST MATTHEW XVI (5–12)

JUAN DE FLANDES (Active 1496; died before 1519)   *Palacio Nacional, Madrid*

("The Miracle of the Loaves and Fishes")

THE FEEDING OF THE FOUR THOUSAND

AND after six days Jesus taketh Peter, James, and John his brother, and bringeth them up into an high mountain apart, and was transfigured before them: and his face did shine as the sun, and his raiment was white as the light. And, behold, there appeared unto them Moses and Elijah talking with him. Then answered Peter, and said unto Jesus:—"Lord, it is good for us to be here; if thou wilt, let us make here three tabernacles; one for thee, and one for Moses, and one for Elijah." While he yet spake, behold, a bright cloud overshadowed them: and behold a voice out of the cloud, which said:—"This is my beloved Son, in whom I am well pleased; hear ye him." And when the disciples heard it, they fell on their face, and were sore afraid. And Jesus came and touched them, and said:—"Arise, and be not afraid." And when they had lifted up their eyes, they saw no man, save Jesus only. And as they came down from the mountain, Jesus charged them, saying:—"Tell the vision to no man, until the Son of Man be risen again from the dead." And his disciples asked him, saying:—"Why then say the scribes that Elijah must first come?" And Jesus answered and said unto them:—"Elijah truly shall first come, and restore all things. But I say unto you, that Elijah is come already, and they knew him not, but have done unto him whatsoever they listed. Likewise shall also the Son of Man suffer of them." Then the disciples understood that he spake unto them of John the Baptist.

And when they were come to the multitude, there came to him a certain man, kneeling down to him, and saying:—"Lord, have mercy on my son: for he is lunatic, and sore vexed: for ofttimes he falleth into the fire, and oft into the water. And I brought him to thy disciples, and they could not cure him." Then Jesus answered and said:—"O faithless and perverse generation, how long shall I be with you? how long shall I suffer you? bring him hither to me." And Jesus rebuked the devil; and he departed out of him: and the child was cured from that very hour. Then came the disciples to Jesus apart, and said:—"Why could not we cast him out?" And Jesus said unto them:—"Because of your unbelief: for verily I say unto you, if ye have faith as a grain of mustard seed, ye shall say unto this mountain, remove hence to yonder place; and it shall remove; and nothing shall be impossible unto you. Howbeit this kind goeth not out but by prayer and fasting."

ST MATTHEW XVII (1–21)

RAPHAEL (1483–1520)

Vatican Gallery, Rome

("The Transfiguration")

THE TRANSFIGURATION,
AND THE DISCIPLES TRYING TO CURE THE BOY

AND while they abode in Galilee, Jesus said unto them:—"The Son of man shall be betrayed unto the hands of men: and they shall kill him, and the third day he shall be raised again." And they were exceeding sorry.

And when they were come to Capernaum, they that received tribute money came to Peter, and said:—"Doth not your master pay tribute?" He saith, "Yes." And when he was come into the house, Jesus presented him, saying:—"What thinkest thou, Simon? of whom do the kings of the earth take custom or tribute? of their own children, or of strangers?" Peter saith unto him:—"Of strangers." Jesus saith unto him:—"Then are the children free. Notwithstanding, lest we should offend them, go thou to the sea, and cast an hook, and take up the fish that first cometh up; and when thou hast opened his mouth, thou shalt find a piece of money: that take, and give unto them for Me and thee."

ST MATTHEW XVII (22–27)

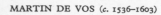
MARTIN DE VOS (c. 1536–1603)

THE TRIBUTE MONEY
FOUND IN THE FISH'S MOUTH

Musée des Beaux-Arts, Antwerp

A T the same time came the disciples unto Jesus, saying:—"Who is the greatest in the kingdom of heaven?" And Jesus called a little child unto him, and set him in the midst of them, and said:—

"Verily I say unto you, except ye be converted, and become as little children, ye shall not enter into the Kingdom of Heaven. Whosoever therefore shall humble himself as this little child, the same is greatest in the kingdom of heaven. And whoso shall receive one such little child in my name receiveth me. But whoso shall offend one of these little ones which believe in me, it were better for him that a millstone were hanged about his neck, and that he were drowned in the depth of the sea. Woe unto the world because of offences! for it must needs be that offences come; but woe to that man by whom the offence cometh!

"Wherefore if thy hand or thy foot offend thee, cut them off, and cast them from thee: it is better for thee to enter into life halt or maimed, rather than having two hands or two feet to be cast into everlasting fire. And if thine eye offend thee, pluck it out, and cast it from thee: it is better for thee to enter into life with one eye, rather than having two eyes to be cast into hell fire.

"Take heed that ye despise not one of these little ones; for I say unto you, that in heaven their angels do always behold the face of my Father which is in heaven. For the Son of man is come to save that which was lost. How think ye? if a man have an hundred sheep, and one of them be gone astray, doth he not leave the ninety and nine, and goeth into the mountains, and seeketh that which is gone astray? And if so be that he find it, verily I say unto you, he rejoiceth more of that sheep, than of the ninety and nine which went not astray. Even so it is not the will of your Father which is in heaven, that one of these little ones should perish."

ST MATTHEW XVIII (1–14)

MEISTER DES HAUSBUCHS (Late XV Century)

("Hovering Angels")

Kunstmuseum, Basel

IN HEAVEN THEIR ANGELS ...

THE UNMERCIFUL SERVANT

THEN came Peter to him, and said:—"Lord, how oft shall my brother sin against me, and I forgive him? till seven times?" Jesus saith unto him:—
"I say not unto thee, Until seven times: but, Until seventy times seven. Therefore is the kingdom of heaven likened unto a certain king, which would take account of his servants. And when he had begun to reckon, one was brought unto him, which owed him ten thousand talents. But forasmuch as he had not to pay, his lord commanded him to be sold, and his wife, and children, and all that he had, and payment to be made. The servant therefore fell down, and worshipped him, saying, Lord, have patience with me, and I will pay thee all. Then the lord of that servant was moved with compassion, and loosed him, and forgave him the debt. But the same servant went out, and found one of his fellowservants, which owed him an hundred pence: and he laid hands on him, and took him by the throat, saying, Pay me that thou owest. And his fellowservant fell down at his feet, and besought him, saying, Have patience with me, and I will pay thee all. And he would not: but went and cast him into prison, till he should pay the debt. So when his fellow-servants saw what was done, they were very sorry, and came and told unto their lord all that was done. Then his lord, after that he had called him, said unto him, O thou wicked servant, I forgave thee all that debt, because thou desiredst me: shouldest not thou also have had compassion on thy fellow-servant, even as I had pity on thee? And his lord was wroth, and delivered him to the tormentors, till he should pay all that was due unto him. So likewise shall my heavenly Father do also unto you, if ye from your hearts forgive not every one his brother their trespasses."

ST MATTHEW XVIII (21–35)

DOMENICO FETI (c. 1589–1624)   *Gemäldegalerie, Dresden*

THE UNMERCIFUL SERVANT

JESUS REBUKES JAMES AND JOHN

AND it came to pass, when the time was come that he should be received up, he stedfastly set his face to go to Jerusalem, and sent messengers before his face: and they went, and entered into a village of the Samaritans, to make ready for him. And they did not receive him, because his face was as though he would go to Jerusalem. And when his disciples James and John saw this, they said:—"Lord, wilt thou that we command fire to come down from heaven, and consume them, even as Elijah did?" But he turned, and rebuked them, and said:—"Ye know not what manner of spirit ye are of. For the Son of man is not come to destroy men's lives, but to save them." And they went to another village.

ST LUKE IX (51–56)

JESUS SHOWS HOW HE IS TO BE FOLLOWED

AND it came to pass, that, as they went in the way, a certain man said unto him:—"Lord, I will follow thee whithersoever thou goest." And Jesus said unto him:—"Foxes have holes, and birds of the air have nests; but the Son of man hath not where to lay his head." And he said unto another:—"Follow me." But he said:—"Lord, suffer me first to go and bury my father." Jesus said unto him:—"Let the dead bury their dead: but go thou and preach the kingdom of God." And another also said:—"Lord, I will follow thee; but let me first go bid them farewell, which are at home at my house." And Jesus said unto him:—"No man, having put his hand to the plough, and looking back, is fit for the kingdom of God."

ST LUKE IX (57–62)

JESUS SENDS OUT SEVENTY DISCIPLES

AFTER these things the Lord appointed other seventy also, and sent them two and two before his face into every city and place, whether he himself would come. Therefore said he unto them:—"The harvest truly is great, but the labourers are few: pray ye therefore the Lord of the harvest, that he would send forth labourers into his harvest. Go your ways: behold, I send you forth as lambs among wolves.

ST LUKE X (I–3)

FROM A FLEMISH BOOK OF HOURS
(*c.* 1510) Attributed to Simon Bening
("Christ Admonishes his Disciples")

I SEND YOU FORTH
AS LAMBS AMONG WOLVES

Courtesy of the Walters Art Gallery,
Baltimore, Maryland

FROM AN ENGLISH MS.
(Second quarter of XII Century)

FOXES HAVE HOLES AND
BIRDS OF THE AIR
HAVE NESTS

British Museum, London

THE WOMAN TAKEN IN ADULTERY

AND early in the morning Jesus came again into the temple, and all the people came unto him; and he sat down, and taught them. And the scribes and Pharisees brought unto him a woman taken in adultery; and when they had set her in the midst, they say unto him:—"Master, this woman was taken in adultery, in the very act. Now Moses in the law commanded us, that such should be stoned: but what sayest thou?" This they said, tempting him, that they might have to accuse him. But Jesus stooped down, and with his finger wrote on the ground, as though he heard them not. So when they continued asking him, he lifted up himself, and said unto them:—"He that is without sin among you, let him first cast a stone at her." And again he stooped down, and wrote on the ground. And they which heard it, being convicted by their own conscience, went out one by one, beginning at the eldest, even unto the last: and Jesus was left alone, and the woman standing in the midst. When Jesus had lifted up himself, and saw none but the woman, he said unto her:— "Woman, where are those thine accusers? hath no man condemned thee?" She said:—"No man, Lord." And Jesus said unto her:—"Neither do I condemn thee: go, and sin no more."

ST. JOHN VIII (2-11)

JESUS AND THE WOMAN TAKEN IN ADULTERY

AND as Jesus passed by, he saw a man which was blind from his birth. And his disciples asked him, saying:—"Master, who did sin, this man, or his parents, that he was born blind?" Jesus answered:—"Neither hath this man sinned, nor his parents: but that the works of God should be made manifest in him. I must work the works of him that sent me, while it is day: the night cometh, when no man can work. As long as I am in the world, I am the light of the world." When he had thus spoken, he spat on the ground, and made clay of the spittle, and he anointed the eyes of the blind man with the clay, and said unto him:—"Go, wash in the pool of Siloam," (which is by interpretation, Sent). He went his way therefore, and washed, and came seeing.

The neighbours therefore, and they which before had seen him that he was blind, said:—"Is not this he that sat and begged?" Some said:—"This is he:" others said:—"He is like him:" but he said:—"I am he." Therefore said they unto him:—"How were thine eyes opened?" He answered and said:—"A man that is called Jesus made clay, and anointed mine eyes, and said unto me, Go to the pool of Siloam, and wash: and I went and washed, and I received sight." Then said they unto him:—"Where is he?" He said:—"I know not."

They brought to the Pharisees him that aforetime was blind. And it was the sabbath day when Jesus made the clay, and opened his eyes. Then again the Pharisees also asked him how he had received his sight. He said unto them:—"He put clay upon mine eyes, and I washed, and do see." Therefore said some of the Pharisees:—"This man is not of God, because he keepeth not the sabbath day." Others said:—"How can a man that is a sinner do such miracles?" And there was a division among them. They say unto the blind man again:—"What sayest thou of him, that he hath opened thine eyes?" He said:—"He is a prophet." But the Jews did not believe concerning him, that he had been blind, and received his sight, until they called the parents of him that had received his sight. And they asked them, saying:—"Is this your son, who ye say was born blind? how then doth he now see?" His parents answered them and said:—"We know that this is our son, and that he was born blind: but by what means he now seeth, we know not; or who hath opened his eyes, we know not: he is of age; ask him: he shall speak for himself." These words spake his parents, because they feared the Jews: for the Jews had agreed already, that if any man did confess that he was Christ, he should be put out of the synagogue. Therefore said his parents:—"He is of age; ask him."

ST. JOHN IX (1–23)

[108]

EL GRECO (1548–1625)

Reale Pinacoteca, Parma

JESUS HEALING A BLIND MAN

THEN again called they the man that was blind, and said unto him:—"Give God the praise: we know that this man is a sinner." He answered and said:—"Whether he be a sinner or no, I know not: one thing I know, that whereas I was blind, now I see." Then said they to him again:—"What did he to thee? how opened he thine eyes?" He answered them:—"I have told you already, and ye did not hear: wherefore would ye hear it again: will ye also be his disciples?" Then they reviled him, and said:—"Thou art his disciple; but we are Moses' disciples. We know that God spake unto Moses: as for this fellow, we know not from whence he is." The man answered and said unto them:—"Why herein is a marvellous thing, that ye know not from whence he is, and yet he hath opened mine eyes. Now we know that God heareth not sinners; but if any man be a worshipper of God, and doeth his will, him he heareth. Since the world began was it not heard that any man opened the eyes of one that was born blind. If this Man were not of God, he could do nothing." They answered and said unto him:—"Thou wast altogether born in sin, and dost thou teach us?" And they cast him out.

Jesus heard that they had cast him out; and when he had found him, he said unto him:—"Dost thou believe on the Son of God?" He answered and said:—"Who is he, Lord, that I might believe on him?" And Jesus said unto him:—"Thou hast both seen him, and it is he that talketh with thee." And he said:—"Lord, I believe." And he worshipped him. And Jesus said:—"For judgment I am come into this world, that they which see not might see; and that they which see might be made blind." And some of the Pharisees which were with him heard these words, and said unto him:—"Are we blind also?" Jesus said unto them:—"If ye were blind, ye should have no sin: but now ye say, We see; therefore your sin remaineth."

ST JOHN IX (24–41)

DUCCIO (c. 1255–c. 1315)   *National Gallery, London*

JESUS HEALING A BLIND MAN

JESUS HEALING A BLIND MAN

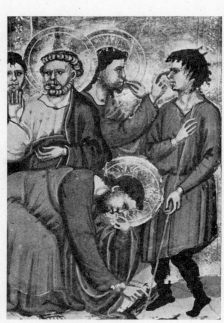

FROM AN ITALO-HUNGARIAN MS. (XIV Century)
Courtesy of the Pierpont Morgan Library, New York

THE GOOD SHEPHERD

"VERILY, verily, I say unto you, He that entereth not by the door into the sheepfold, but climbeth up some other way, the same is a thief and a robber. But he that entereth in by the door is the shepherd of the sheep. To him the porter openeth; and the sheep hear his voice: and he calleth his own sheep by name, and leadeth them out. And when he putteth forth his own sheep, he goeth before them, and the sheep follow him: for they know his voice. And a stranger will they not follow, but will flee from him: for they know not the voice of strangers." This parable spake Jesus unto them, but they understood not what things they were which he spake unto them.

Then said Jesus unto them again:—"Verily, verily, I say unto you, I am the door of the sheep. All that ever came before me are thieves and robbers: but the sheep did not hear them. I am the door: by me if any man enter in, he shall be saved, and shall go in and out, and find pasture. The thief cometh not, but for to steal, and to kill, and to destroy: I am come that they might have life, and that they might have it more abundantly.

"I am the good shepherd: the good shepherd giveth his life for the sheep. But he that is an hireling, and not the shepherd, whose own the sheep are not, seeth the wolf coming, and leaveth the sheep, and fleeth: and the wolf catcheth them, and scattereth the sheep. The hireling fleeth, because he is an hireling, and careth not for the sheep. I am the good shepherd, and know my sheep, and am known of mine. As the Father knoweth me, even so know I the Father: and I lay down my life for the sheep. And other sheep I have, which are not of this fold: them also I must bring, and they shall hear my voice; and there shall be one fold, and one shepherd. Therefore doth my Father love me, because I lay down my life, that I might take it again. No man taketh it from me, but I lay it down of myself. I have power to lay it down, and I have power to take it again. This commandment have I received of my Father."

There was a division therefore again among the Jews for these sayings. And many of them said:—"He hath a devil, and is mad; why hear ye him?" Others said:—"These are not the words of him that hath a devil. Can a devil open the eyes of the blind?"

ST JOHN X (I–21)

[112]

P. BREUGHEL THE ELDER (c. 1525–70)

THE HIRELING SHEPHERD

AND the seventy returned again with joy, saying:—"Lord, even the devils are subject unto us through thy name." And he said unto them:—"I beheld Satan as lightning fall from heaven. Behold, I give unto you power to tread on serpents and scorpions, and over all the power of the enemy: and nothing shall by any means hurt you. Notwithstanding in this rejoice not, that the spirits are subject unto you; but rather rejoice, because your names are written in heaven." In that hour Jesus rejoiced in spirit, and said:—"I thank thee, O Father, Lord of heaven and earth, that thou hast hid these things from the wise and prudent, and hast revealed them unto babes: even so, Father; for so it seemed good in thy sight. All things are delivered to me of my Father and no man knoweth who the Son is, but the Father; and who the Father is, but the Son, and he to whom the Son will reveal him." And he turned him unto his disciples, and said privately:—"Blessed are the eyes which see the things that ye see: for I tell you, that many prophets and kings have desired to see those things which ye see, and have not seen them; and to hear those things which ye hear, and have not heard them."

ST LUKE X (17–24)

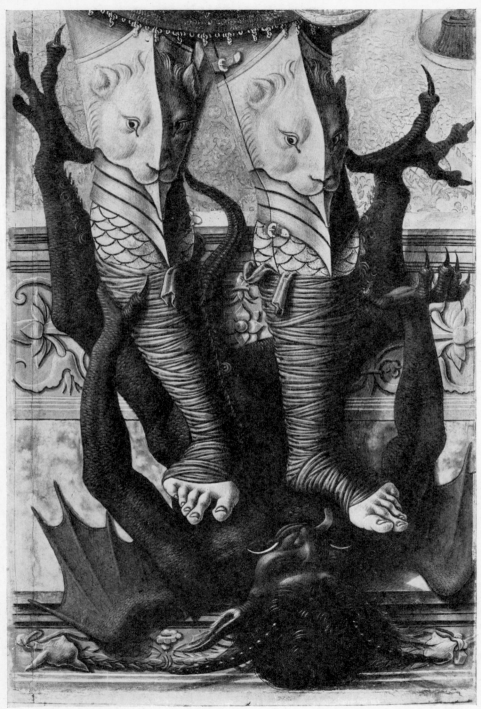

CRIVELLI (1430?–93?)   *National Gallery, London*

(A detail from "The Demidoff Altarpiece")

EVEN THE DEVILS ARE SUBJECT UNTO US
THROUGH THY NAME

THE GOOD SAMARITAN

AND, behold, a certain lawyer stood up, and tempted him, saying:—"Master, what shall I do to inherit eternal life?" He said unto him:—"What is written in the law? how readest thou?" And he answering said:—"Thou shalt love the Lord thy God with all thy heart, and with all thy soul, and with all thy strength, and with all thy mind; And thy neighbour as thyself." And he said unto him:—"Thou hast answered right: this do, and thou shalt live." But he, willing to justify himself, said unto Jesus:—"And who is my neighbour?" And Jesus answering said:—"A certain man went down from Jerusalem to Jericho, and fell among thieves, which stripped him of his raiment, and wounded him, and departed, leaving him half dead. And by chance there came down a certain priest that way: and when he saw him, he passed by on the other side. And likewise a Levite, when he was at the place, came and looked on him, and passed by on the other side. But a certain Samaritan, as he journeyed, came where he was: and when he saw him, he had compassion on him, and went to him, and bound up his wounds, pouring in oil and wine, and set him on his own beast, and brought him to an inn, and took care of him. And on the morrow when he departed, he took out two pence, and gave them to the host, and said unto him, Take care of him; and whatsoever thou spendest more, when I come again, I will repay thee. Which now of these three, thinkest thou, was neighbour unto him that fell among the thieves?" And he said:—"He that shewed mercy on him." Then said Jesus unto him:—"Go, and do thou likewise."

ST LUKE X (25–37)

J. BASSANO (1510–92)

THE GOOD SAMARITAN

REMBRANDT (1607–69)
Wallace Collection, London

NOW it came to pass, as they went, that he entered into a certain village: and a certain woman named Martha received him into her house. And she had a sister called Mary, which also sat at Jesus' feet, and heard his word. But Martha was cumbered about much serving, and came to him, and said:— "Lord, dost thou not care that my sister hath left me to serve alone? bid her therefore that she help me." And Jesus answered and said unto her: "Martha, Martha, thou art careful and troubled about many things: but one thing is needful: and Mary hath chosen that good part, which shall not be taken away from her."

ST LUKE X (38–42)

JESUS IN THE HOUSE OF MARTHA AND MARY

AND he was casting out a devil, and it was dumb. And it came to pass, when the devil was gone out, the dumb spake; and the people wondered. But some of them said:—"He casteth out devils through Beelzebub the chief of the devils." And others, tempting him, sought of him a sign from heaven. But he, knowing their thoughts, said unto them:—"Every kingdom divided against itself is brought to desolation; and a house divided against a house falleth. If Satan also be divided against himself, how shall his kingdom stand? because ye say that I cast out devils through Beelzebub. And if I by Beelzebub cast out devils, by whom do your sons cast them out? therefore shall they be your judges. But if I with the finger of God cast out devils, no doubt the kingdom of God is come upon you. When a strong man armed keepeth his palace, his goods are in peace: but when a stronger than he shall come upon him, and overcome him, he taketh from him all his armour wherein he trusted, and divideth his spoils. He that is not with me is against me: and he that gathereth not with me scattereth. When the unclean spirit is gone out of a man, he walketh through dry places, seeking rest; and finding none, he saith, I will return unto my house whence I came out. And when he cometh, he findeth it swept and garnished. Then goeth he, and taketh to him seven other spirits more wicked than himself; and they enter in, and dwell there: and the last state of that man is worse than the first."

And it came to pass, as he spake these things, a certain woman of the company lifted up her voice, and said unto him:—"Blessed is the womb that bare thee, and the paps which thou hast sucked." But he said:—"Yea, rather, blessed are they that hear the word of God, and keep it."

ST LUKE XI (14–28)

THE SCRIBES AND PHARISEES ASK FOR A SIGN

THEN certain of the scribes and of the Pharisees answered, saying:—"Master, we would see a sign from thee." But he answered and said unto them:—"An evil and adulterous generation seeketh after a sign; and there shall no sign be given to it, but the sign of the prophet Jonah: for as Jonah was three days and three nights in the whale's belly; so shall the Son of man be three days and three nights in the heart of the earth. The men of Nineveh shall rise in judgment with this generation, and shall condemn it: because they repented at the preaching of Jonah; and, behold, a greater than Jonah is here. The queen of the south shall rise up in the judgment with this generation, and shall condemn it: for she came from the uttermost parts of the earth to hear the wisdom of Solomon; and, behold, a greater than Solomon is here."

ST MATTHEW XII (38–42)

FROM THE PRAYER BOOK OF RENÉ DE LORRAINE
(French; end of XV Century)

Cabinet des Manuscrits,
Bibliothèque Nationale, Paris

JONAH CAST INTO THE SEA

JESUS WARNS AGAINST COVETOUSNESS

AND one of the company said unto him:—"Master, speak to my brother, that he divide the inheritance with me." And he said unto him:—"Man, who made me a judge or a divider over you?" And he said unto them:—"Take heed, and beware of covetousness: for a man's life consisteth not in the abundance of the things which he possesseth." And he spake a parable unto them, saying:—"The ground of a certain rich man brought forth plentifully: and he thought within himself, saying, What shall I do, because I have no room where to bestow my fruits? And he said, This will I do: I will pull down my barns, and build greater; and there will I bestow all my fruits and my goods. And I will say to my soul, Soul, thou hast much goods laid up for many years; take thine ease, eat, drink, and be merry. But God said unto him, Thou fool, this night thy soul shall be required of thee: then whose shall those things be, which thou hast provided? So is he that layeth up treasure for himself, and is not rich toward God."

ST LUKE XII (13–21)

THE TREASURE THAT FAILETH NOT

SELL that ye have, and give alms; provide yourselves bags which wax not old, A treasure in the heavens that faileth not, Where no thief approacheth, neither moth corrupteth. For where your treasure is, there will your heart be also.

ST LUKE XII (33–34)

HANS FRIES (c. 1465–c. 1520)   Cordeliers, Fribourg
(A detail from "The Death of the Miser")

WHERE YOUR TREASURE IS,
THERE WILL YOUR HEART BE ALSO

JESUS SPEAKS OF REPENTANCE

THERE were present at that season some that told him of the Galilæans, whose blood Pilate had mingled with their sacrifices. And Jesus answering said unto them:—"Suppose ye that these Galilæans were sinners above all the Galilæans, because they suffered such things? I tell you, nay: but, except ye repent, ye shall all likewise perish. Or those eighteen, upon whom the tower in Siloam fell, and slew them, think ye that they were sinners above all men that dwelt in Jerusalem? I tell you, nay: but, except ye repent, ye shall all likewise perish."

ST LUKE XIII (1-5)

THE PARABLE OF THE FIG TREE

HE spake also this parable:—"A certain man had a fig tree planted in his vineyard; and he came and sought fruit thereon, and found none. Then said he unto the dresser of his vineyard, Behold, these three years I come seeking fruit on this fig tree, and find none: cut it down; why cumbereth it the ground? And he answering said unto him, Lord, let it alone this year also, till I shall dig about it, and dung it: and if it bear fruit, well: and if not, then after that thou shalt cut it down."

ST LUKE XIII (6-9)

JESUS HEALS AN INFIRM WOMAN

AND he was teaching in one of the synagogues on the sabbath. And, behold, there was a woman which had a spirit of infirmity eighteen years, and was bowed together, and could in no wise lift up herself. And when Jesus saw her, he called her to him, and said unto her:—"Woman, thou art loosed from thine infirmity." And he laid his hands on her: and immediately she was made straight, and glorified God. And the ruler of the synagogue answered with indignation, because that Jesus had healed on the sabbath day, and said unto the people:—"There are six days in which men ought to work: in them therefore come and be healed, and not on the sabbath day." The Lord then answered him, and said:—"Thou hypocrite, doth not each one of you on the sabbath loose his ox or his ass from the stall, and lead him away to watering? And ought not this woman, being a daughter of Abraham, whom Satan hath bound, lo, these eighteen years, be loosed from this bond on the sabbath day?" And when he had said these things, all his adversaries were ashamed: and all the people rejoiced for all the glorious things that were done by him.

ST LUKE XIII (10-17)

MOSAIC OF THE XII CENTURY   *Cathedral, Monreale*

JESUS HEALING AN INFIRM WOMAN

DISCOURSES AT THE FEAST OF THE DEDICATION

AND it was at Jerusalem the feast of the dedication, and it was winter. And Jesus walked in the temple in Solomon's porch. Then came the Jews round about him, and said unto him:—"How long dost thou make us to doubt? If thou be the Christ, tell us plainly." Jesus answered them:—"I told you, and ye believed not: the works that I do in my Father's name, they bear witness of me. But ye believe not, because ye are not of my sheep, as I said unto you. My sheep hear my voice, and I know them, and they follow me: and I give unto them eternal life; and they shall never perish, neither shall any man pluck them out of my hand. My Father, which gave them me, is greater than all; and no man is able to pluck them out of my Father's hand. I and my Father are one." Then the Jews took up stones again to stone him. Jesus answered them:—"Many good works have I shewed you from my Father; for which of those works do ye stone me?" The Jews answered him, saying:—"For a good work we stone thee not; but for blasphemy, and because that thou, being a man, makest thyself God." Jesus answered them:—"Is it not written in your law, I said, Ye are gods? If he called them gods, unto whom the word of God came, and the scripture cannot be broken; say ye of him, whom the Father hath sanctified, and sent into the world, Thou blasphemest; because I said, I am the Son of God? If I do not the works of my Father, believe me not. But if I do, though ye believe not me, believe the words: that ye may know, and believe, that the Father is in me, and I in him." Therefore they sought again to take him: but he escaped out of their hand.

ST JOHN X (22–39)

JESUS HEALS A MAN WITH A DROPSY

AND it came to pass, as he went into the house of one of the chief Pharisees to eat bread on the sabbath day, that they watched him. And, behold, there was a certain man before him which had the dropsy. And Jesus answering spake unto the lawyers and Pharisees, saying:—"Is it lawful to heal on the sabbath day?" And they held their peace. And he took him, and healed him, and let him go; and answered them, saying:—"Which of you shall have an ass or an ox fallen into a pit, and will not straightway pull him out on the sabbath day?" And they could not answer him again to these things.

ST LUKE XIV (1–6)

FROM THE BREVIARY OF ISABELLA,
QUEEN OF SPAIN (End of XV Century)

THE JEWS
TAKE UP STONES

British Museum, London

FROM AN ARMENIAN MS. OF THE GOSPEL
(XIII Century)

JESUS HEALING THE MAN
WITH THE DROPSY

Courtesy of the Freer Gallery of Art, Smithsonian
Institution, Washington, D.C.

AND he put forth a parable to those which were bidden, when he marked how they chose out the chief rooms; saying unto them:—"When thou art bidden of any man to a wedding, sit not down in the highest room; lest a more honourable man than thou be bidden of him; and he that bade thee and him come and say to thee, Give this man place; and thou begin with shame to take the lowest room. But when thou art bidden, go and sit down in the lowest room; that when he that bade thee cometh, he may say unto thee, Friend, go up higher: then shalt thou have worship in the presence of them that sit at meat with thee. For whosoever exalteth himself shall be abased; and he that humbleth himself shall be exalted." Then said he also to him that bade him:—"When thou makest a dinner or a supper, call not thy friends, nor thy brethren, neither thy kinsmen, nor thy rich neighbours; lest they also bid thee again, and a recompense be made thee. But when thou makest a feast, call the poor, the maimed, the lame, the blind: and thou shalt be blessed; for they cannot recompense thee: for thou shalt be recompensed at the resurrection of the just."

ST LUKE XIV (7–14)

THE GREAT SUPPER

AND when one of them that sat at meat with him heard these things, he said unto him:—"Blessed is he that shall eat bread in the kingdom of God." Then said he unto him:—"A certain man made a great supper, and bade many: and sent his servant at supper time to say to them that were bidden, Come; for all things are now ready. And they all with one consent began to make excuse. The first said unto him, I have bought a piece of ground, and I must needs go and see it: I pray thee have me excused. And another said, I have bought five yoke of oxen, and I go to prove them: I pray thee have me excused. And another said, I have married a wife, and therefore I cannot come. So that servant came, and shewed his lord these things. Then the master of the house being angry said to his servant, Go out quickly into the streets and lanes of the city, and bring in hither the poor, and the maimed, and the halt, and the blind. And the servant said, Lord, it is done as thou hast commanded, and yet there is room. And the lord said unto the servant, Go out into the highways and hedges, and compel them to come in, that my house may be filled. For I say unto you, that none of those men which were bidden shall taste of my supper."

ST LUKE XIV (15–24)

FROM THE CODEX AUREUS (German; *c.* 1045)   *Monastery of San Lorenzo el Real, Escorial, Madrid*

THE GREAT SUPPER

AND there went great multitudes with him: and he turned, and said unto them:—"If any man come to me, and hate not his father, and mother, and wife, and children, and brethren, and sisters, yea, and his own life also, he cannot be my disciple. And whosoever doth not bear his cross, and come after me, cannot be my disciple. For which of you, intending to build a tower, sitteth not down first, and counteth the cost, whether he have sufficient to finish it? Lest haply, after he hath laid the foundation, and is not able to finish it, all that behold it begin to mock him, saying, This man began to build, and was not able to finish. Or what king, going to make war against another king, sitteth not down first, and consulteth whether he be able with ten thousand to meet him that cometh against him with twenty thousand? Or else, while the other is yet a great way off, he sendeth an ambassage, and desireth conditions of peace. So likewise, whosoever he be of you that forsaketh not all that he hath, he cannot be my disciple."

ST LUKE XIV (25–33)

THE LOST SHEEP AND THE LOST PIECE OF SILVER

THEN drew near unto him all the publicans and sinners for to hear him. And the Pharisees and scribes murmured, saying:—"This man receiveth sinners, and eateth with them." And he spake this parable unto them, saying:—"What man of you, having an hundred sheep, if he lose one of them, doth not leave the ninety and nine in the wilderness, and go after that which is lost, until he find it? And when he hath found it, he layeth it on his shoulders, rejoicing. And when he cometh home, he calleth together his friends and neighbours, saying unto them, Rejoice with me; for I have found my sheep which was lost. I say unto you, that likewise joy shall be in heaven over one sinner that repenteth, more than over ninety and nine just persons, which need no repentance. Either what woman having ten pieces of silver, if she lose one piece, doth not light a candle, and sweep the house, and seek diligently till she find it? And when she hath found it, she calleth her friends and her neighbours together, saying, Rejoice with me; for I have found the piece which I had lost. Likewise, I say unto you, there is joy in the presence of the angels of God over one sinner that repenteth."

ST LUKE XV (1–10)

T. GADDI (Died before 1366)

S. Croce, Florence

(A detail from "The Meeting of St. Joachim and St. Anna")

THE LOST SHEEP

THE PRODIGAL SON

AND he said:—"A certain man had two sons: and the younger of them said to his father, Father, give me the portion of goods that falleth to me. And he divided unto them his living. And not many days after the younger son gathered all together, and took his journey into a far country, and there wasted his substance with riotous living. And when he had spent all, there arose a mighty famine in that land; and he began to be in want. And he went and joined himself to a citizen of that country; and he sent him into his fields to feed swine. And he would fain have filled his belly with the husks that the swine did eat: and no man gave unto him. And when he came to himself, he said, How many hired servants of my father's have bread enough and to spare, and I perish with hunger! I will arise and go to my father, and will say unto him, Father, I have sinned against heaven, and before thee, and am no more worthy to be called thy son: make me as one of thy hired servants. And he arose, and came to his father. But when he was yet a great way off, his father saw him, and had compassion, and ran, and fell on his neck, and kissed him. And the son said unto him, Father, I have sinned against heaven, and in thy sight, and am no more worthy to be called thy son. But the father said to his servants, Bring forth the best robe, and put it on him; and put a ring on his hand, and shoes on his feet: and bring hither the fatted calf, and kill it; and let us eat, and be merry: for this my son was dead, and is alive again; he was lost, and is found. And they began to be merry. Now his elder son was in the field: and as he came and drew nigh to the house, he heard music and dancing. And he called one of the servants, and asked what these things meant. And he said unto him, Thy brother is come; and thy father hath killed the fatted calf, because he hath received him safe and sound. And he was angry, and would not go in: therefore came his father out, and intreated him. And he answering said to his father, Lo, these many years do I serve thee, neither transgressed I at any time thy commandment: and yet thou never gavest me a kid, that I might make merry with my friends: but as soon as this thy son was come, which hath devoured thy living with harlots, thou hast killed for him the fatted calf. And he said unto him, Son thou art ever with me, and all that I have is thine. It was meet that we should make merry, and be glad: for this thy brother was dead, and is alive again; and was lost, and is found."

ST LUKE XV (11–32)

[132]

BOSCH (1460?–1518)

Boymans Museum, Rotterdam

THE PRODIGAL SON

THE RICH MAN AND LAZARUS

"THERE was a certain rich man, which was clothed in purple and fine linen, and fared sumptuously every day: and there was a certain beggar named Lazarus, which was laid at his gate, full of sores, and desiring to be fed with the crumbs which fell from the rich man's table: moreover the dogs came and licked his sores. And it came to pass, that the beggar died, and was carried by the angels into Abraham's bosom: the rich man also died, and was buried; and in hell he lift up his eyes, being in torments, and seeth Abraham afar off, and Lazarus in his bosom. And he cried and said, Father Abraham, have mercy on me, and send Lazarus that he may dip the tip of his finger in water, and cool my tongue; for I am tormented in this flame. But Abraham said, Son, remember that thou in thy lifetime receivedst thy good things, and likewise Lazarus evil things: but now he is comforted, and thou art tormented. And beside all this, between us and you there is a great gulf fixed: so that they which would pass from hence to you cannot: neither can they pass to us, that would come from thence. Then he said, I pray thee therefore, father, that thou wouldest send him to my father's house: for I have five brethren; that he may testify unto them, lest they also come into this place of torment. Abraham saith unto him, They have Moses and the prophets: let them hear them. And he said, Nay, father Abraham: but if one went unto them from the dead, they will repent. And he said unto him, If they hear not Moses and the prophets, neither will they be persuaded, though one rose from the dead."

ST LUKE XVI (19–31)

FAITH AND DUTY

AND the Apostles said unto the Lord:—"Increase our faith." And the Lord said:—"If ye had faith like as a grain of mustard seed, ye might say unto this sycamine tree, Be thou plucked up by the root, and be thou planted in the sea; and it should obey you.

"But which of you, having a servant plowing or feeding cattle, will say unto him by and by, when he is come from the field, Go and sit down to meat, and will not rather say unto him, Make ready wherewith I may sup, and gird thyself, and serve me, till I have eaten and drunken; and afterward thou shalt eat and drink? Doth he thank that servant because he did the things that were commanded him? I trow not. So likewise ye, when ye shall have done all those things which are commanded you, say, We are unprofitable servants: we have done that which was our duty to do."

ST LUKE XVII (5–10)

BERNAERT VAN ORLEY (c. 1492–1542)

THE RICH MAN AND LAZARUS

NOW a certain man was sick, named Lazarus, of Bethany, the town of Mary and her sister Martha. (It was that Mary which anointed the Lord with ointment, and wiped his feet with her hair, whose brother Lazarus was sick.) Therefore his sisters sent unto him, saying:—"Lord, behold, he whom thou lovest is sick." When Jesus heard that, he said:—"This sickness is not unto death, but for the glory of God, that the Son of God might be glorified thereby." Now Jesus loved Martha, and her sister, and Lazarus. When he had heard therefore that he was sick, he abode two days still in the same place where he was. Then after that saith he to his disciples:—"Let us go into Judæa again." His disciples say unto him :—"Master, the Jews of late sought to stone thee; and goest thou thither again?" Jesus answered:—"Are there not twelve hours in the day? If any man walk in the day, he stumbleth not, because he seeth the light of this world. But if a man walk in the night, he stumbleth, because there is no light in him." These things said he: and after that he saith unto them:—"Our friend Lazarus sleepeth; but I go, that I may awake him out of sleep." Then said his disciples:—"Lord, if he sleep, he shall do well." Howbeit Jesus spake of his death: but they thought that he had spoken of taking of rest in sleep. Then said Jesus unto them plainly:—"Lazarus is dead. And I am glad for your sakes that I was not there, to the intent ye may believe; nevertheless let us go unto him." Then said Thomas, which is called Didymus, unto his fellow-disciples:—"Let us also go, that we may die with him."

Then when Jesus came, he found that he had laid in the grave four days already. Now Bethany was nigh unto Jerusalem, about fifteen furlongs off: and many of the Jews came to Martha and Mary, to comfort them concerning their brother. Then Martha, as soon as she heard that Jesus was coming, went and met him: but Mary sat still in the house. Then said Martha unto Jesus:— "Lord, if thou hadst been here, my brother had not died. But I know, that even now, whatsoever thou wilt ask of God, God will give it thee." Jesus saith unto her:—"Thy brother shall rise again." Martha saith unto him:—"I know that he shall rise again in the resurrection at the last day." Jesus said unto her:—"I am the resurrection, and the life: he that believeth in me, though he were dead, yet shall he live: and whosoever liveth and believeth in me shall never die. Believest thou this?" She saith unto him:—"Yea, Lord: I believe that thou art the Christ, the Son of God, which should come into the world."

ST JOHN XI (1–27)

GEERTGEN TOT SINT JANS (Late XV Century) *Louvre, Paris*

THE RAISING OF LAZARUS

AND when she had so said, she went her way, and called Mary her sister secretly, saying:—"The Master is come, and calleth for thee." As soon as she heard that, she arose quickly, and came unto him. Now Jesus was not yet come into the town, but was in that place where Martha met him. The Jews then which were with her in the house, and comforted her, when they saw Mary, that she rose up hastily and went out, followed her, saying, "She goeth unto the grave to weep there." Then when Mary was come where Jesus was, and saw him, she fell down at his feet, saying unto him:—"Lord, if thou hadst been here, my brother had not died." When Jesus therefore saw her weeping, and the Jews also weeping which came with her, he groaned in the spirit, and was troubled, and said:—"Where have ye laid him?" They said unto him:—"Lord, come and see." Jesus wept. Then said the Jews:— "Behold how he loved him!" And some of them said:—"Could not this man, which opened the eyes of the blind, have caused that even this man should not have died?" Jesus therefore again groaning in himself cometh to the grave. It was a cave, and a stone lay upon it. Jesus said:—"Take ye away the stone." Martha, the sister of him that was dead, saith unto him:—"Lord, by this time he stinketh: for he hath been dead four days." Jesus saith unto her:—"Said I not unto thee, that, if thou wouldest believe, thou shouldest see the glory of God?" Then they took away the stone from the place where the dead was laid. And Jesus lifted up his eyes, and said:—"Father, I thank thee that thou hast heard me. And I knew that thou hearest me always: but because of the people which stand by I said it, that they may believe that thou hast sent me." And when he thus had spoken, he cried with a loud voice:—"Lazarus, come forth." And he that was dead came forth, bound hand and foot with graveclothes: and his face was bound about with a napkin. Jesus saith unto them:—"Loose him, and let him go." Then many of the Jews which came to Mary, and had seen the things which Jesus did, believed on him.

ST JOHN XI (28–45)

GIOTTO (1266–1337)

Arena Chapel, Padua

THE RAISING OF LAZARUS

BUT some of them went their ways to the Pharisees, and told them what things Jesus had done.

Then gathered the chief priests and the Pharisees a council, and said:—"What do we? for this man doeth many miracles. If we let him thus alone, all men will believe on him: and the Romans shall come and take away both our place and nation." And one of them, named Caiaphas, being the high priest that same year, said unto them:—"Ye know nothing at all, nor consider that it is expedient for us, that one man should die for the people, and that the whole nation perish not." And this spake he not of himself: but being high priest that year, he prophesied that Jesus should die for that nation; and not for that nation only, but that also he should gather together in one the children of God that were scattered abroad. Then from that day forth they took council together for to put him to death.

Jesus therefore walked no more openly among the Jews; but went thence unto a country near to the wilderness, into a city called Ephraim, and there continued with his disciples. And the Jews' passover was nigh at hand: and many went out of the country up to Jerusalem before the passover, to purify themselves. Then sought they for Jesus, and spake among themselves, as they stood in the temple:—"What think ye, that he will not come to the feast?" Now both the chief priests and the Pharisees had given a commandment, that, if any man knew where he were, he should shew it, that they might take him.

ST JOHN XI (46–57)

JESUS HEALS TEN LEPERS

AND it came to pass, as he went to Jerusalem, that he passed through the midst of Samaria and Galilee. And as he entered into a certain village, there met him ten men that were lepers, which stood afar off: and they lifted up their voices, and said, "Jesus, Master, have mercy on us." And when he saw them, he said unto them:—"Go shew yourselves unto the priests." And it came to pass, that, as they went, they were cleansed. And one of them, when he saw that he was healed, turned back, and with a loud voice glorified God, and fell down on his face at his feet, giving him thanks: and he was a Samaritan. And Jesus answering said:—"Were there not ten cleansed? but where are the nine? There are not found that returned to give glory to God, save this stranger." And he said unto him:—"Arise, go thy way: thy faith hath made thee whole."

ST LUKE XVII (11–19)

F. PARMEGIANINO (1503–40)
(A copy by N. dell'Abbate: 1512–71)

*From the Devonshire Collection (reproduced by
permission of the Chatsworth Estates Company)*

JESUS HEALING TEN LEPERS

FROM AN ARMENIAN MS. OF THE GOSPEL
(XIII Century)

JESUS HEALING TEN LEPERS

*Courtesy of the Freer Gallery of Art, Smithsonian
Institution, Washington, D.C.*

THE COMING OF THE KINGDOM OF GOD

AND when he was demanded of the Pharisees, when the kingdom of God should come, he answered them and said:—"The kingdom of God cometh not with observation: neither shall they say, Lo here! or, lo there! for behold, the kingdom of God is within you." And he said unto the disciples:—"The days will come, when ye shall desire to see one of the days of the Son of man, and ye shall not see it. And they shall say to you, See here; or, see there: go not after them, nor follow them. For as the lightning, that lighteneth out of the one part under heaven, shineth unto the other part under heaven; so shall also the Son of man be in his day. But first must he suffer many things, and be rejected of this generation. And as it was in the days of Noah, so shall it be also in the days of the Son of man. They did eat, they drank, they married wives, they were given in marriage, until the day that Noah entered into the ark, and the flood came, and destroyed them all. Likewise also as it was in the days of Lot; they did eat, they drank, they bought, they sold, they planted, they builded; but the same day that Lot went out of Sodom it rained fire and brimstone from heaven, and destroyed them all. Even thus shall it be in the day when the Son of man is revealed. In that day, he which shall be upon the housetop, and his stuff in the house, let him not come down to take it away: and he that is in the field, let him likewise not return back. Remember Lot's wife. Whosoever shall seek to save his life shall lose it; and whosoever shall lose his life shall preserve it."

ST LUKE XVII (20–33)

THE PHARISEE AND THE PUBLICAN

AND he spake this parable unto certain which trusted in themselves that they were righteous, and despised others:—"Two men went up into the temple to pray; the one a Pharisee, and the other a publican. The Pharisee stood and prayed thus with himself, God, I thank thee, that I am not as other men are, extortioners, unjust, adulterers, or even as this publican. I fast twice in the week, I give tithes of all that I possess. And the publican, standing afar off, would not lift up so much as his eyes unto heaven, but smote upon his breast, saying, God be merciful to me a sinner. I tell you, this man went down to his house justified rather than the other: for every one that exalteth himself shall be abased; and he that humbleth himself shall be exalted."

ST LUKE XVIII (9–14)

.. BASSANO (1558–1623)   *Private Collection, Venice*

NOAH'S ARK

THE PHARISEE AND THE PUBLICAN

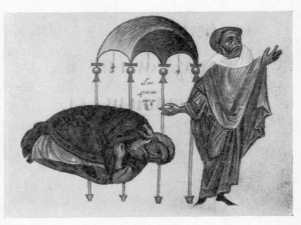

AND they brought young children to him, that he should touch them: and his disciples rebuked those that brought them. But when Jesus saw it, he was much displeased, and said unto them:—"Suffer the little children to come unto me, and forbid them not: for of such is the kingdom of God. Verily I say unto you, Whosoever shall not receive the kingdom of God as a little child, he shall not enter therein." And he took them up in his arms, put his hands upon them, and blessed them.

ST MARK X (13–16)

THE RICH YOUNG MAN

AND when he was gone forth into the way, there came one running, and kneeled to him, and asked him:—"Good Master, what shall I do that I may inherit eternal life?" And Jesus said unto him:—"Why callest thou me good? there is none good but one, that is, God. Thou knowest the commandments, Do not commit adultery. Do not kill. Do not steal. Do not bear false witness. Defraud not. Honour thy father and mother." And he answered and said unto him:—"Master, all these have I observed from my youth."

Then Jesus beholding him, loved him, and said unto him:—"One thing thou lackest, go thy way, sell whatsoever thou hast, and give to the poor, and thou shalt have treasure in heaven: and come, take up the cross, and follow me." And he was sad at that saying, and went away grieved: for he had great possessions. And Jesus looked round about, and saith unto his disciples:— "How hardly shall they that have riches enter into the kingdom of God!" And the disciples were astonished at his words. But Jesus answereth again, and saith unto them:—"Children, how hard is it for them that trust in riches to enter into the kingdom of God! It is easier for a camel to go through the eye of a needle, than for a rich man to enter into the kingdom of God." And they were astonished out of measure, saying among themselves, who then can be saved? And Jesus looking upon them saith:—"With men it is impossible, but not with God: for with God all things are possible." Then Peter began to say unto him:—"Lo, we have left all, and have followed thee." And Jesus answered and said:—"Verily I say unto you, there is no man that hath left house, or brethren, or sisters, or father, or mother, or wife, or children, or lands, for my sake, and the gospel's, but he shall receive an hundredfold now in this time, houses, and brethren, and sisters, and mothers, and children, and lands, with persecutions; and in the world to come eternal life."

ST MARK X (17–30)

SCHOOL OF REMBRANDT   *National Gallery, London*

JESUS BLESSING A CHILD

THE LABOURERS IN THE VINEYARD

''BUT many that are first shall be last; and the last shall be first. For the kingdom of heaven is like unto a man that is an householder, which went out early in the morning to hire labourers into his vineyard. And when he had agreed with the labourers for a penny a day, he sent them into his vineyard. And he went out about the third hour, and saw others standing idle in the market place, and said unto them; Go ye also into the vineyard, and whatsoever is right I will give you. And they went their way. Again he went out about the sixth and ninth hour, and did likewise. And about the eleventh hour he went out, and found others standing idle, and saith unto them, Why stand ye here all the day idle? They say unto him, Because no man hath hired us. He saith unto them, Go ye also into the vineyard; and whatsoever is right, that shall ye receive. So when even was come, the lord of the vineyard saith unto his steward, Call the labourers, and give them their hire, beginning from the last unto the first. And when they came that were hired about the eleventh hour, they received every man a penny. But when the first came, they supposed that they should have received more; and they likewise received every man a penny. And when they had received it, they murmured against the goodman of the house, saying, These last have wrought but one hour, and thou hast made them equal unto us, which have borne the burden and heat of the day. But he answered one of them, and said, Friend, I do thee no wrong: didst not thou agree with me for a penny? Take that thine is, and go thy way: I will give unto this last, even as unto thee. Is it not lawful for me to do what I will with mine own? Is thine eye evil, because I am good? So the last shall be first, and the first last: for many be called, but few chosen.''

ST MATTHEW XIX (30)
ST MATTHEW XX (1–16)

DOMENICO FETI (c. 1589–1624)   *Gemäldegalerie, Dresden*

THE HOUSEHOLDER AND THE LABOURER

JESUS HEALS TWO BLIND MEN OF JERICHO

AND as they departed from Jericho, a great multitude followed him. And, behold, two blind men sitting by the way side, when they heard that Jesus passed by, cried out, saying:—"Have mercy on us, O Lord, thou son of David." And the multitude rebuked them, because they should hold their peace: but they cried the more, saying:—"Have mercy on us, O Lord, thou son of David." And Jesus stood still, and called them, and said:—"What will ye that I shall do unto you?" They say unto him:—"Lord, that our eyes may be opened." So Jesus had compassion on them, and touched their eyes: and immediately their eyes received sight, and they followed Him.

ST MATTHEW XX (29–34)

ZACCHÆUS

AND Jesus entered and passed through Jericho. And, behold, there was a man named Zacchæus, which was the chief among the publicans, and he was rich. And he sought to see Jesus who he was; and could not for the press, because he was little of stature. And he ran before, and climbed up into a sycamore tree to see him: for he was to pass that way. And when Jesus came to the place he looked up, and saw him, and said unto him:—"Zacchæus, make haste, and come down; for today I must abide at thy house." And he made haste, and came down, and received him joyfully. And when they saw it, they all murmured, saying, that he was gone to be guest with a man that is a sinner. And Zacchæus stood, and said unto the Lord:—"Behold, Lord, the half of my goods I give to the poor; and if I have taken anything from any man by false accusation, I restore him fourfold." And Jesus said unto him:—"This day is salvation come to this house, forsomuch as he also is a son of Abraham. For the Son of man is come to seek and to save that which was lost."

ST LUKE XIX (1–10)

[148]

N. POUSSIN (1594–1665)

Louvre, Paris

JESUS HEALING THE TWO BLIND MEN OF JERICHO

ZACCHÆUS IN THE SYCAMORE TREE

FROM THE BREVIARY OF RAINALD IV, DUKE OF GUELDRES (Dutch: *c.* 1415)

Courtesy of the Pierpont Morgan Library, New York

THEN Jesus six days before the passover came to Bethany, where Lazarus was which had been dead, whom he raised from the dead. There they made him a supper; and Martha served: but Lazarus was one of them that sat at the table with him. Then took Mary a pound of ointment of spikenard, very costly, and anointed the feet of Jesus, and wiped his feet with her hair: and the house was filled with the odour of the ointment. Then saith one of his disciples, Judas Iscariot, Simon's son, which should betray him:—"Why was not this ointment sold for three hundred pence, and given to the poor?" This he said, not that he cared for the poor; but because he was a thief, and had the bag, and bare what was put therein. Then said Jesus:—"Let her alone: against the day of my burying hath she kept this. For the poor always ye have with you: but me ye have not always."

Much people of the Jews therefore knew that he was there: and they came not for Jesus' sake only, but they might see Lazarus also, whom he had raised from the dead. But the chief priests consulted that they might put Lazarus also to death; because that by reason of him many of the Jews went away, and believed on Jesus.

ST JOHN XII (I–II)

MORETTO DA BRESCIA (c. 1498–1554)　　　　　　　　　　　　　　　　　　*S. Maria del Pieta, Venice*

(Central portion of "The Supper in the Pharisee's House")

MARY ANOINTING JESUS' FEET

JESUS RIDES INTO JERUSALEM

AND when they came nigh to Jerusalem, unto Bethphage and Bethany, at the mount of Olives, he sendeth forth two of his disciples, and saith unto them:—"Go your way into the village over against you: and as soon as ye be entered into it, ye shall find a colt tied, whereon never man sat; loose him, and bring him. And if any man say unto you, Why do ye this? ye say that the Lord hath need of him; and straightway he will send him hither." And they went their way, and found the colt tied by the door without in a place where two ways met; and they loose him. And certain of them that stood there said unto them, "What do ye, loosing the colt?" And they said unto them even as Jesus had commanded: and they let them go. And they brought the colt to Jesus, and cast their garments on him; and he sat upon him. And many spread their garments in the way: and others cut down branches off the trees, and strawed them in the way. And they that went before, and they that followed, cried, saying:—"Hosanna: Blessed is he that cometh in the name of the Lord: Blessed be the kingdom of our father David, that cometh in the name of the Lord: Hosanna in the highest." And Jesus entered into Jerusalem, and into the temple: and when he had looked round about upon all things, and now the eventide was come, he went out unto Bethany with the twelve.

And on the morrow, when they were come from Bethany, he was hungry; and seeing a fig tree afar off having leaves, he came, if haply he might find any thing thereon: and when he came to it, he found nothing but leaves; for the time of figs was not yet. And Jesus answered and said unto it:—"No man eat fruit of thee hereafter for ever." And his disciples heard it.

ST MARK XI (1–14)

JESUS PURGES THE TEMPLE A SECOND TIME

AND they come to Jerusalem: and Jesus went into the temple, and began to cast out them that sold and bought in the temple, and overthrew the tables of the moneychangers, and the seats of them that sold doves; and would not suffer that any man should carry any vessel through the temple. And he taught, saying unto them:—"Is it not written, my house shall be called of all nations the house of prayer? But ye have made it a den of thieves." And the scribes and chief priests heard it, and sought how they might destroy him: for they feared him, because all the people were astonished at his teaching. And when even was come, he went out of the city.

ST MARK XI (15–19)

GIOTTO (1266–1337)   *Arena Chapel, Padua*

JESUS RIDING INTO JERUSALEM

THE WITHERED FIG TREE

AND in the morning, as they passed by, they saw the fig tree dried up from the roots. And Peter calling to remembrance said unto him:—"Master, behold, the fig tree which thou cursedst is withered away." And Jesus answering saith unto them:—"Have faith in God. For verily I say unto you, that whosoever shall say unto this mountain, Be thou removed, and be thou cast into the sea; and shall not doubt in his heart, but shall believe that those things which he saith shall come to pass; he shall have whatsoever he saith. Therefore I say unto you, what things soever ye desire, when ye pray, believe that ye receive them, and ye shall have them. And when ye stand praying, forgive, if ye have ought against any: that your Father also which is in heaven may forgive you your trespasses. But if ye do not forgive, neither will your Father which is in heaven forgive your trespasses."

ST MARK XI (20–26)

THE AUTHORITY OF JESUS

AND they come again to Jerusalem: and as he was walking in the temple, there come to him the chief priests and the scribes, and the elders, and say unto him:—"By what authority doest thou these things? and who gave thee this authority to do these things?" And Jesus answered and said unto them:— "I will also ask of you one question, and answer me, and I will tell you by what authority I do these things. The baptism of John, was it from heaven, or of men? answer me." And they reasoned with themselves, saying, If we shall say, from heaven; he will say, Why then did ye not believe him? But if we shall say, of men; they feared the people: for all men counted John, that he was a prophet indeed. And they answered and said unto Jesus:—"We cannot tell." And Jesus answering saith unto them:—"Neither do I tell you by what authority I do these things."

ST MARK XI (27–33)

RUBENS (1577–1640)

(A detail from "The Woman taken in Adultery")

Musée Royal, Brussels

TWO JEWISH PRIESTS QUESTIONING JESUS

THE TWO SONS

"BUT what think ye? A certain man had two sons; and he came to the first, and said, Son, go work today in my vineyard. He answered and said, I will not: but afterward he repented, and went. And he came to the second, and said likewise. And he answered and said, I go, sir: and went not. Whether of them twain did the will of his father?" They said unto him, "The first." Jesus saith unto them:—"Verily I say unto you, that the publicans and the harlots go into the kingdom of God before you. For John came unto you in the way of righteousness, and ye believed him not: but the publicans and the harlots believed him: and ye, when ye had seen it, repented not afterward, that ye might believe him."

ST MATTHEW XXI (28–32)

THE WICKED HUSBANDMEN

"HEAR another parable: There was a certain householder, which planted a vineyard, and hedged it round about, and digged a winepress in it, and built a tower, and let it out to husbandmen, and went into a far country: and when the time of fruit drew near, he sent his servants to the husbandmen, that they might receive the fruits of it. And the husbandmen took his servants, and beat one, and killed another, and stoned another. Again, he sent other servants more than the first: and they did unto them likewise. But last of all he sent unto them his son, saying, They will reverence my son. But when the husbandmen saw the son, they said among themselves, This is the heir; come, let us kill him, and let us seize on his inheritance. And they caught him, and cast him out of the vineyard, and slew him. When the lord thereof of the vineyard cometh, what will he do unto those husbandmen?"

They say unto him, "He will miserably destroy those wicked men, and will let out his vineyard unto other husbandmen, which shall render him the fruits in their seasons." Jesus saith unto them:—

"Did ye never read in the scriptures, The stone which the builders rejected, The same is become the head of the corner: This is the Lord's doing, and it is marvellous in our eyes? Therefore say I unto you, the kingdom of God shall be taken from you, and given to a nation bringing forth the fruits thereof. And whosoever shall fall on this stone shall be broken: but on whomsoever it shall fall, it will grind him to powder."

And when the chief priests and Pharisees had heard his parables, they perceived that he spake of them. But when they sought to lay hands on him, they feared the multitude, because they took him for a prophet.

ST MATTHEW XXI (33–46)

FROM A MORALISED BIBLE HISTORY (French; end of XIII Century)   *British Museum, London*

THE WICKED HUSBANDMEN

TRIBUTE TO CÆSAR

THEN went the Pharisees, and took counsel how they might entangle him in his talk. And they sent out unto him their disciples with the Herodians, saying:—"Master, we know that thou art true, and teachest the way of God in truth, neither carest thou for any man: for thou regardest not the person of men. Tell us therefore, What thinkest thou? Is it lawful to give tribute unto Cæsar, or not?" But Jesus perceived their wickedness, and said:—"Why tempt ye me, ye hypocrites? Shew me the tribute money." And they brought unto him a penny. And he saith unto them:—"Whose is this image and superscription?" They say unto him, "Cæsar's." Then saith he unto them:— "Render therefore unto Cæsar the things which are Cæsar's; and unto God the things that are God's." When they had heard these words, they marvelled, and left him, and went their way.

ST MATTHEW XXII (15–22)

THE RESURRECTION OF THE DEAD

THEN come unto him the Sadducees, which say there is no resurrection; and they asked him, saying:—"Master, Moses wrote unto us, if a man's brother die, and leave his wife behind him, and leave no children, that his brother should take his wife, and raise up seed unto his brother. Now there were seven brethren: and the first took a wife, and dying left no seed. And the second took her, and died, neither left he any seed: and the third likewise. And the seven had her, and left no seed: last of all the woman died also. In the resurrection therefore, when they shall rise, whose wife shall she be of them, for the seven had her to wife?" And Jesus answering said unto them:—"Do ye not therefore err, because ye know not the scriptures, neither the power of God? For when they shall rise from the dead, they neither marry, nor are given in marriage; but are as the angels which are in heaven. And as touching the dead, that they rise: have ye not read in the book of Moses, how in the bush God spake unto him, saying, I am the God of Abraham, and the God of Isaac, and the God of Jacob? He is not the God of the dead, but the God of the living, ye therefore do greatly err."

ST MARK XII (18–27)

TITIAN (1477–1576)   Gemäldegalerie, Dresden

("Christ and the Money")

WHOSE IS THIS IMAGE AND SUPERSCRIPTION?

THE FIRST COMMANDMENT

AND one of the scribes came, and having heard them reasoning together, and perceiving that he had answered them well, asked him:—"Which is the first commandment of all?" And Jesus answered him:—"The first of all the commandments is, Hear, O Israel: The Lord our God is one Lord: Thou shalt love the Lord thy God with all they heart, And with all thy soul, and with all thy mind, and with all thy strength; This is the first commandment. And the second is like, namely, this, Thou shalt love thy neighbour as thyself. There is none other commandment greater than these." And the scribe said unto him:—"Well, Master, thou hast said the truth: for there is one God; and there is none other but he: and to love him with all the heart, and with all the understanding, and with all the soul, and with all the strength, and to love his neighbour as himself, is more than all whole burnt offerings and sacrifices." And when Jesus saw that he answered discreetly, he said unto him:—"Thou art not far from the kingdom of God." And no man after that durst ask him any question.

ST MARK XII (28–34)

THE WIDOW'S MITE

AND Jesus sat over against the treasury, and beheld how the people cast money into the treasury: and many that were rich cast in much. And there came a certain poor widow, and she threw in two mites, which make a farthing. And he called unto him his disciples, and saith unto them:—"Verily I say unto you, that this poor widow hath cast more in, than all they which have cast into the treasury: for all they did cast in of their abundance; but she of her want did cast in all that she had, even all her living."

ST MARK XII (41–44)

THE WIDOW'S MITE

Musée des Beaux-Arts, Antwerp

"THEN shall the kingdom of heaven be likened unto ten virgins, which took their lamps, and went forth to meet the bridegroom. And five of them were wise, and five were foolish. They that were foolish took their lamps, and took no oil with them: but the wise took oil in their vessels with their lamps. While the bridegroom tarried, they all slumbered and slept. And at midnight there was a cry made, Behold, the bridegroom cometh; go ye out to meet him. Then all those virgins arose, and trimmed their lamps. And the foolish said unto the wise, Give us of your oil; for our lamps are gone out. But the wise answered, saying, Not so; lest there be not enough for us and you: but go ye rather to them that sell, and buy for yourselves. And while they went to buy, the bridegroom came; and they that were ready went in with him to the marriage: and the door was shut. Afterward came also the other virgins, saying, Lord, Lord, open to us. But he answered and said, Verily I say unto you, I know you not. Watch therefore, for ye know neither the day nor the hour wherein the Son of man cometh."

ST MATTHEW XXV (1–13)

THE WISE AND FOOLISH VIRGINS

JUDAS SELLS JESUS TO THE CHIEF PRIESTS

AND it came to pass, when Jesus had finished all these sayings, he said unto his disciples:—"Ye know that after two days is the feast of the passover, and the Son of man is betrayed to be crucified."

Then assembled together the chief priests, and the scribes, and the elders of the people, unto the palace of the high priest, who was called Caiaphas, and consulted that they might take Jesus by subtilty, and kill him. But they said, "Not on the feast day, lest there be an uproar among the people."

Then one of the twelve, called Judas Iscariot, went unto the chief priests, and said unto them, What will ye give me, and I will deliver him unto you? And they covenanted with him for thirty pieces of silver. And from that time he sought opportunity to betray him.

ST MATTHEW XXVI (1–5; 14–16)

THE DISCIPLES PREPARE THE PASSOVER

NOW the first day of the feast of the unleavened bread the disciples came to Jesus, saying unto him:—"Where wilt thou that we prepare for thee to eat the passover?" And he said:—"Go into the city to such a man, and say unto him, The Master saith, My time is at hand; I will keep the passover at thy house with my disciples." And the disciples did as Jesus had appointed them; and they made ready the passover.

ST MATTHEW XXVI (17–19)

THE GREATEST OF THE APOSTLES

AND when the hour was come, he sat down, and the twelve apostles with him.

And there was also a strife among them, which of them should be accounted the greatest. And he said unto them:—"The kings of the Gentiles exercise lordship over them; and they that exercise authority upon them are called benefactors. But ye shall not be so: but he that is greatest among you, let him be as the younger: and he that is chief, as he that doth serve. For whether is greater, he that sitteth at meat, or he that serveth? is not he that sitteth at meat? but I am among you as he that serveth. Ye are they which have continued with me in my temptations. And I appoint unto you a kingdom, as my Father hath appointed unto me; that ye may eat and drink at my table in my kingdom, and sit on thrones judging the twelve tribes of Israel."

ST LUKE XXII (14; 24–30)

FRA ANGELICO (1387–1455)   *Museo di S. Marco, Florence*

JUDAS SELLING JESUS

JESUS WASHES THE DISCIPLES' FEET

AND at* supper, the devil having now put into the heart of Judas Iscariot, Simon's son, to betray him; Jesus knowing that the Father had given all things into his hands, and that he was come from God, and went to God; he riseth from supper, and laid aside his garments; and took a towel, and girded himself. After that he poureth water into a bason, and began to wash the disciples' feet, and to wipe them with the towel wherewith he was girded. Then cometh he to Simon Peter: and Peter saith unto him:—"Lord, dost thou wash my feet?" Jesus answered and said unto him:—"What I do thou knowest not now; but thou shalt know hereafter." Peter saith unto him:—"Thou shalt never wash my feet." Jesus answered him:—"If I wash thee not, thou hast no part with me." Simon Peter saith unto him:—"Lord, not my feet only, but also my hands and my head." Jesus saith to him:—"He that is washed needeth not save to wash his feet, but is clean every whit: and ye are clean, but not all." For he knew who should betray him; therefore said he, "Ye are not all clean." So after he had washed their feet, and had taken his garments, and was set down again, he said unto them:—"Know ye what I have done to you? Ye call me Master and Lord: and ye say well; for so I am. If I then, your Lord and Master, have washed your feet; ye also ought to wash one another's feet. For I have given you an example, that ye should do as I have done to you. Verily, verily, I say unto you, the servant is not greater than his lord; neither he that is sent greater than he that sent him. If ye know these things, happy are ye if ye do them. I speak not of you all: I know whom I have chosen: but that the scripture may be fulfilled, He that eateth bread with me hath lifted up his heel against me. Now I tell you before it come, that, when it is come to pass, ye may believe that I am he. Verily, verily, I say unto you, he that receiveth whomsoever I send receiveth me; and he that receiveth me receiveth him that sent me."

ST JOHN XIII (2–20)

* *According to modern translators, the washing of feet took place during, rather than after supper.* (E. H.)

[166]

FORD MADOX BROWN (1821–93)

National Gallery, London

JESUS WASHING PETER'S FEET

WHEN Jesus had thus said, he was troubled in spirit, and testified, and said:—"Verily, verily, I say unto you, that one of you shall betray me." Then the disciples looked one on another, doubting of whom he spake. Now there was leaning on Jesus' bosom one of his disciples, whom Jesus loved. Simon Peter therefore beckoned to him, that he should ask who it should be of whom he spake. He then lying on Jesus' breast saith unto him:—"Lord, who is it?" Jesus answered:—"He it is, to whom I shall give a sop, when I have dipped it." And when he had dipped the sop, he gave it to Judas Iscariot, the son of Simon. And after the sop Satan entered into him. Then said Jesus unto him:—"That thou doest, do quickly." Now no man at the table knew for what intent he spake this unto him. For some of them thought, because Judas had the bag, that Jesus had said unto him, Buy those things that we have need of against the feast; or, that he should give something to the poor. He then having received the sop went immediately out: and it was night.

ST JOHN XIII (21–30)

THE INSTITUTION OF THE EUCHARIST

THEREFORE, when he was gone out, Jesus said:—"Now is the Son of man glorified, and God is glorified in him. If God be glorified in him, God shall also glorify him in himself, and shall straightway glorify him. Little children, yet a little while I am with you. Ye shall seek me: and as I said unto the Jews, whither I go, ye cannot come; so now I say to you. A new commandment I give unto you, that ye love one another; as I have loved you, that ye also love one another. By this shall all men know that ye are my disciples, if ye have love one to another."

ST JOHN XIII (31–35)

And as they were eating, Jesus took bread, and blessed it, and brake it, and gave it to the disciples, and said:—"Take eat; this is my body." And he took the cup, and gave thanks, and gave it to them, saying:—"Drink ye all of it; for this is my blood of the new testament, which is shed for many for the remission of sins. But I say unto you, I will not drink henceforth of this fruit of the vine, until that day when I drink it new with you in my Father's kingdom."

ST MATTHEW XXVI (26–29)

DIERIC BOUTS (1400?–75)   *St. Pierre, Louvain*

THE LAST SUPPER

"IF ye love me, keep my commandments. And I will pray the Father, and he shall give you another Comforter, that he may abide with you for ever; even the Spirit of truth; whom the world cannot receive, because it seeth him not, neither knoweth him: but ye know him; for he dwelleth with you, and shall be in you. I will not leave you comfortless: I will come to you. Yet a little while, and the world seeth me no more; but ye see me: because I live, ye shall live also. At that day ye shall know that I am in my Father, and ye in me, and I in you. He that hath my commandments, and keepeth them, he it is that loveth me: and he that loveth me shall be loved of my Father, and I will love him, and will manifest myself to him."

Judas saith unto him, not Iscariot:—"Lord, how is it that thou wilt manifest thyself unto us, and not unto the world?" Jesus answered and said unto him:— "If a man love me he will keep my words: and my Father will love him, and we will come unto him, and make our abode with him. He that loveth me not keepeth not my sayings: and the word which ye hear is not mine, but the Father's which sent me.

"These things have I spoken unto you, being yet present with you. But the Comforter, which is the Holy Ghost, whom the Father will send in my name, he shall teach you all things, and bring all things to your remembrance, whatsoever I have said unto you. Peace I leave with you, my peace I give unto you: not as the world giveth, give I unto you. Let not your heart be troubled, neither let it be afraid. Ye have heard how I said unto you, I go away, and come again unto you. If ye loved me, ye would rejoice, because I said, I go unto the Father: for my Father is greater than I. And now I have told you before it come to pass, that, when it is come to pass, ye might believe. Hereafter I will not talk much with you: for the prince of this world cometh, and hath nothing in me. But that the world may know that I love the Father; and as the Father gave me commandment, even so I do. Arise, let us go hence."

ST JOHN XIV (15-31)

[170]

SIGNORELLI (1441–1523)   *Ducal Palace, Urbino*

THE DESCENT OF THE HOLY GHOST

THE COMMANDMENT TO LOVE ONE ANOTHER

"THESE things have I spoken unto you, that my joy might remain in you, and that your joy might be full. This is my commandment, that ye love one another, as I have loved you. Greater love hath no man than this, that a man lay down his life for his friends. Ye are my friends, if ye do whatsoever I command you. Henceforth I call you not servants; for the servant knoweth not what his lord doeth: but I have called you friends; for all things that I have heard of my Father I have made known unto you. Ye have not chosen me, but I have chosen you, and ordained you, that ye should go and bring forth fruit, and that your fruit should remain: that whatsoever ye shall ask of the Father in my name, He may give it you. These things I command you, that ye love one another."

ST JOHN XV (11–17)

WHAT THE DISCIPLES MUST EXPECT OF THE WORLD

"IF the world hate you, ye know that it hated me before it hated you. If ye were of the world, the world would love his own: but because ye are not of the world, but I have chosen you out of the world, therefore the world hateth you. Remember the word that I said unto you, The servant is not greater than his lord. If they have persecuted me, they will also persecute you: if they have kept my saying, they will keep yours also. But all these things will they do unto you for my name's sake, because they know not him that sent me. If I had not come and spoken unto them, they had not had sin: but now they have no cloak for their sin. He that hateth me hateth my Father also. If I had not done among them the works which none other man did, they had not had sin: but now have they both seen and hated both me and my Father. But this cometh to pass, that the word might be fulfilled that is written in their law, They hated me without a cause. But when the Comforter is come whom I will send unto you from the Father, even the Spirit of truth, which proceedeth from the Father, he shall testify of me: and ye also shall bear witness, because ye have been with me from the beginning.

"These things have I spoken unto you, that ye should not be offended. They shall put you out of the synagogues: yea, the time cometh, that whosoever killeth you will think that he doeth God service. And these things will they do unto you, because they have not known the Father, nor me. But these things have I told you, that when the time shall come, ye may remember that I told you of them. And these things I said not unto you at the beginning, because I was with you."

ST JOHN XV (18–27)
ST JOHN XVI (1–4)

("Our Lord bidding Farewell to his Mother")
GERARD DAVID (Active 1484; died 1523)

THESE THINGS I
COMMAND YOU . . .

*Courtesy of the
National Gallery of Ireland, Dublin*

JESUS FORETELLS PETER'S DENIAL

WHEN Jesus had spoken these words, he went forth with his disciples over the brook Cedron, where was a garden, into the which he entered, and his disciples. And Judas also, which betrayed him, knew the place: for Jesus ofttimes resorted thither with his disciples.

ST JOHN XVIII (1–2)

And the Lord said, "Simon, Simon, behold, Satan hath desired to have you, that he may sift you as wheat: but I have prayed for thee, that thy faith fail not: and when thou art converted, strengthen thy brethren." And he said unto him, "Lord, I am ready to go with thee, both into prison, and to death." And he said, "I tell thee, Peter, the cock shall not crow this day, before that thou shalt thrice deny that thou knowest me."

And he said unto them, "When I sent you without purse, and scrip, and shoes, lacked ye any thing?" And they said, "Nothing." Then said he unto them, "But now, he that hath a purse, let him take it, and likewise his scrip: and he that hath no sword, let him sell his garment, and buy one. For I say unto you, that this that is written must yet be accomplished in me. And he was reckoned among the transgressors: for the things concerning me have an end." And they said, "Lord, behold, here are two swords." And he said unto them, "It is enough."

ST LUKE XXII (31–38)

KONRAD WITZ (First half of XV Century)   *Musée d'Art et d'Histoire, Geneva*

PETER DELIVERED OUT OF PRISON

THEN cometh Jesus with them unto a place called Gethsemane, and saith unto the disciples, "Sit ye here while I go and pray yonder." And he took with him Peter and the two sons of Zebedee, and began to be sorrowful and very heavy. Then saith he unto them:—"My soul is exceeding sorrowful, even unto death: tarry ye here, and watch with me." And he went a little farther, and fell on his face, and prayed, saying:—"O My Father, if it be possible, let this cup pass from me: nevertheless not as I will, but as thou wilt." And he cometh unto the disciples, and findeth them asleep, and saith unto Peter:—"What, could ye not watch with me one hour? Watch and pray, that ye enter not into temptation: the spirit indeed is willing, but the flesh is weak." He went away again the second time, and prayed, saying:—"O my Father, if this cup may not pass away from me, except I drink it, thy will be done." And he came and found them asleep again: for their eyes were heavy. And he left them, and went away again, and prayed the third time, saying the same words. Then cometh he to his disciples, and saith unto them:—"Sleep on now, and take your rest: behold, the hour is at hand, and the Son of man is betrayed into the hands of sinners. Rise, let us be going: behold, he is at hand that doth betray me."

ST MATTHEW XXVI (36–46)

MANTEGNA (1431-1506)

National Gallery, London

THE AGONY IN THE GARDEN

AND while he yet spake, lo, Judas, one of the twelve, came, and with him a great multitude with swords and staves, from the chief priests and elders of the people. Now he that betrayed him gave them a sign, saying, "Whomsoever I shall kiss, that same is he: hold him fast." And forthwith he came to Jesus, and said, "Hail, master"; and kissed him. And Jesus said unto him:—"Friend, wherefore art thou come?" Then came they, and laid hands on Jesus, and took him. And, behold, one of them which were with Jesus stretched out his hand, and drew his sword, and struck a servant of the high priest's, and smote off his ear. Then said Jesus unto him:—"Put up again thy sword into his place: for all they that take the sword shall perish with the sword. Thinkest thou that I cannot now pray to my Father, and he shall presently give me more than twelve legions of angels? But how then shall the scriptures be fulfilled, that thus it must be?"

In that same hour said Jesus to the multitudes:—"Are ye come out as against a thief with swords and staves for to take me? I sat daily with you teaching in the temple, and ye laid no hold on me. But all this was done, that the scriptures of the prophets might be fulfilled."

Then all the disciples forsook him, and fled.

ST MATTHEW XXVI (47–56)

DIERIC BOUTS (1400?–75)   *Alte Pinakothek, Munich*

THE ARREST OF JESUS

JESUS IS BROUGHT BEFORE ANNAS

THEN the band and the captain and officers of the Jews took Jesus, and bound him, and led him away to Annas first; for he was father in law to Caiaphas, which was the high priest that same year. Now Caiaphas was he, which gave counsel to the Jews, that it was expedient that one man should die for the people.

ST JOHN XVIII (12–14)

JESUS IS BROUGHT BEFORE CAIAPHAS

AND they that had laid hold on Jesus led him away to Caiaphas the high priest, where the scribes and the elders were assembled. But Peter followed him afar off unto the high priest's palace, and went in, and sat with the servants, to see the end. Now the chief priests, and elders, and all the council, sought false witness against Jesus, to put him to death; but found none: yea, though many false witnesses came, yet found they none. At the last came two false witnesses, and said:—"This fellow said, I am able to destroy the temple of God, and to build it in three days." And the high priest arose, and said unto him:— "Answerest thou nothing? what is it which these witness against thee?" But Jesus held his peace. And the high priest answered and said unto him:— "I adjure thee by the living God, that thou tell us whether thou be the Christ, Son of God." Jesus saith unto him:—"Thou hast said: nevertheless I say unto you, Hereafter shall ye see the Son of man sitting on the right hand of power, and coming in the clouds of heaven." Then the high priest rent his clothes, saying:—"He hath spoken blasphemy; what further need have we of witnesses? behold, now ye have heard his blasphemy. What think ye?" They answered and said, "He is guilty of death." Then did they spit in his face, and buffeted him; and others smote him with the palms of their hands, saying, "Prophesy unto us, thou Christ, Who is he that smote thee?"

ST MATTHEW XXVI (57–67)

HANS HOLBEIN THE YOUNGER (1497–1543)   *Kunstmuseum, Basel*

JESUS BEFORE CAIAPHAS

PETER DENIES JESUS

NOW Peter sat without in the palace: and a damsel came unto him, saying:—
"Thou also wast with Jesus of Galilee." But he denied before them all, saying:
—"I know not what thou sayest." And when he was gone out into the porch,
another maid saw him, and said unto them that were there:—"This fellow
was also with Jesus of Nazareth." And again he denied with an oath:—"I do
not know the man." And after a while came unto him they that stood by, and
said to Peter:—"Surely thou also art one of them; for thy speech bewrayeth
thee." Then began he to curse and to swear, saying:—"I know not the man."
And immediately the cock crew. And Peter remembered the word of Jesus,
which said unto him, "Before the cock crow, thou shalt deny me thrice."
And he went out, and wept bitterly.

ST MATTHEW XXVI (69–75)

JUDAS HANGS HIMSELF

WHEN the morning was come, all the chief priests and elders of the people
took counsel against Jesus to put him to death: and when they had bound
him, they led him away, and delivered him to Pontius Pilate the governor.

Then Judas, which had betrayed him, when he saw that he was condemned, repented himself, and brought again the thirty pieces of silver to the
chief priests and elders, saying:—"I have sinned in that I have betrayed the
innocent blood." And they said:—"What is that to us? see thou to that." And
he cast down the pieces of silver in the temple, and departed, and went and
hanged himself. And the chief priests took the silver pieces, and said, "It is
not lawful for to put them into the treasury, because it is the price of blood."
And they took counsel, and bought with them the potter's field, to bury
strangers in. Wherefore that field was called, "The field of blood," unto this
day. Then was fulfilled that which was spoken by Jeremiah the prophet,
saying, And they took the thirty pieces of silver, the price of him that was
valued, whom they of the children of Israel did value; and gave them for the
potter's field, as the Lord appointed me.

ST MATTHEW XXVII (1–10)

[182]

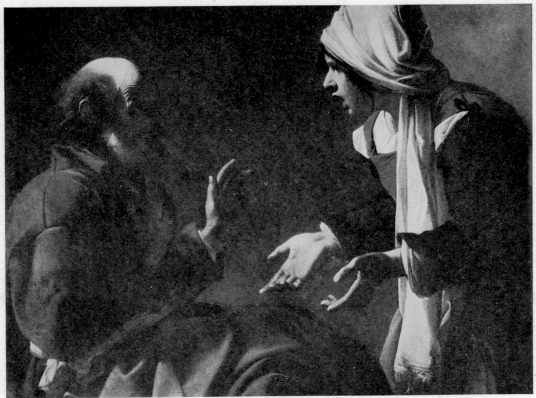

CARAVAGGIO (c. 1560–1609)   *Vatican Gallery, Rome*

PETER DENIES JESUS

FROM AN ITALO-HUNGARIAN MS. (XIV Century)

JUDAS HANGS HIMSELF

Courtesy of the Pierpont Morgan Library, New York

JESUS IS BROUGHT BEFORE PILATE

THEN Pilate entered into the judgment hall again, and called Jesus, and said unto him:—"Art thou the King of the Jews?" Jesus answered him:—"Sayest thou this thing of thyself, or did others tell it thee of me?" Pilate answered:—"Am I a Jew? Thine own nation and the chief priests have delivered thee unto me: what hast thou done?" Jesus answered:—"My kingdom is not of this world: if my kingdom were of this world, then would my servants fight, that I should not be delivered to the Jews: but now is my kingdom not from hence." Pilate therefore said unto him:—"Art thou a king then?" Jesus answered:—"Thou sayest that I am a king. To this end was I born, and for this cause came I into the world, that I should bear witness unto the truth. Every one that is of the truth heareth my voice." Pilate saith unto him:—"What is truth?" And when he had said this, he went out again unto the Jews, and saith unto them:—"I find in him no fault at all."

ST JOHN XVIII (33–38)

JESUS IS BROUGHT BEFORE HEROD

AND they were the more fierce, saying:—"He stirreth up the people, teaching throughout all Jewry, beginning from Galilee to this place." When Pilate heard of Galilee, he asked whether the man were a Galilæan. And as soon as he knew that he belonged to Herod's jurisdiction, he sent him to Herod, who himself was also at Jerusalem at that time. And when Herod saw Jesus, he was exceeding glad: for he was desirous to see him of a long season, because he had heard many things of him; and he hoped to have seen some miracle done by him. Then he questioned with him in many words; but he answered him nothing. And the chief priests and scribes stood and vehemently accused him. And Herod with his men of war set him at nought, and mocked him, and arrayed him in a gorgeous robe, and sent him again to Pilate. And the same day Pilate and Herod were made friends together: for before they were at enmity between themselves.

ST LUKE XXIII (5–12)

[184]

J. FOUQUET (*c. 1420–c. 1480*)   *Musée Condé, Chantilly*

JESUS BEFORE PILATE

JESUS BEFORE PILATE AGAIN

NOW at that feast the governor was wont to release unto the people a prisoner, whom they would. And they had then a notable prisoner, called Barabbas. Therefore when they were gathered together, Pilate said unto them:—"Whom will ye that I release unto you? Barabbas, or Jesus which is called Christ?" For he knew that for envy they had delivered him. When he was set down on the judgment seat, his wife sent unto him, saying:—"Have thou nothing to do with that just man: for I have suffered many things this day in a dream because of Him." But the chief priests and elders persuaded the multitude that they should ask Barabbas, and destroy Jesus. The governor answered and said unto them:—"Whether of the twain will ye that I release unto you?" They said, Barabbas. Pilate saith unto them:—"What shall I do then with Jesus which is called Christ?" They all say unto him:—"Let him be crucified." And the governor said:—"Why, what evil hath he done?" But they cried out the more, saying:—"Let him be crucified." When Pilate saw that he could prevail nothing, but that rather a tumult was made, he took water, and washed his hands before the multitude, saying:—"I am innocent of the blood of this just person: see ye to it." Then answered all the people, and said:—"His blood be on us, and on our children."

ST MATTHEW XXVII (15–25)

JESUS IS CROWNED WITH THORNS

THEN Pilate therefore took Jesus, and scourged him. And the soldiers platted a crown of thorns, and put it on his head, and they put on him a purple robe, and said:—"Hail, King of the Jews!" and they smote him with their hands.

ST JOHN XIX (1–3)

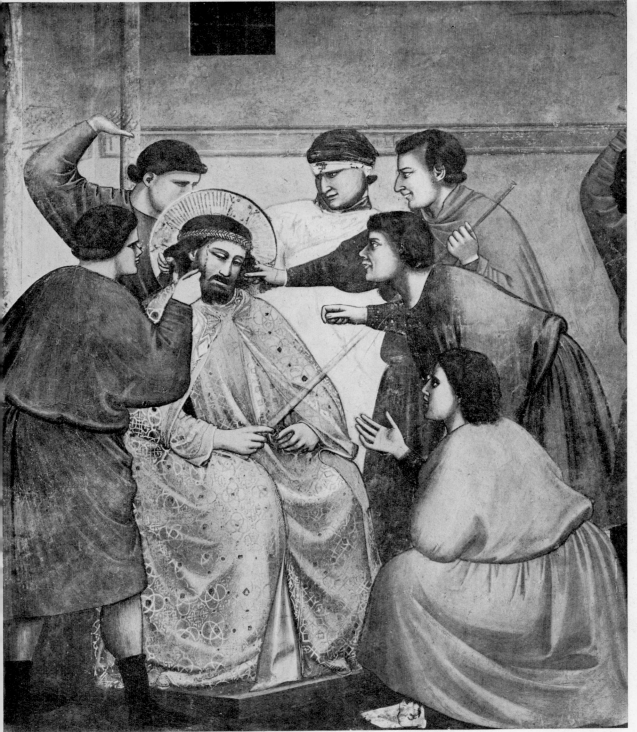

GIOTTO (1266–1337)

Arena Chapel, Padua

(A detail from "Jesus mocked")

JESUS MOCKED BY THE SOLDIERS

JESUS IS DELIVERED TO BE CRUCIFIED

PILATE therefore went forth again, and saith unto them:—"Behold, I bring him forth to you, that ye may know that I find no fault in him." Then came Jesus forth, wearing the crown of thorns, and the purple robe. And Pilate saith unto them:— "Behold the man!" When the chief priests therefore and officers saw him, they cried out, saying:—"Crucify him, crucify him." Pilate saith unto them:—"Take ye him, and crucify him: for I find no fault in him." The Jews answered him:—"We have a law, and by our law he ought to die, because he made himself the Son of God." When Pilate therefore heard that saying, he was the more afraid; and went again into the judgment hall, and saith unto Jesus:—"Whence art Thou?" But Jesus gave him no answer. Then saith Pilate unto him:—"Speakest thou not unto me? knowest thou not that I have power to crucify thee, and have power to release thee?" Jesus answered:—"Thou couldest have no power at all against me, except it were given thee from above: therefore he that delivered me unto thee hath the greater sin." And from thenceforth Pilate sought to release him: but the Jews cried out, saying:—"If thou let this man go, thou art not Cæsar's friend: whosoever maketh himself a king speaketh against Cæsar."

When Pilate therefore heard that saying, he brought Jesus forth, and sat down in the judgment seat in a place that is called the Pavement, but in the Hebrew, Gabbatha. And it was the preparation of the passover, and about the sixth hour: and he saith unto the Jews:—"Behold your King!" But they cried out:—"Away with him, away with him, crucify him." Pilate saith unto them:—"Shall I crucify your King?" The chief priests answered:—"We have no king but Cæsar." Then delivered he him therefore unto them to be crucified. And they took Jesus, and led him away.

ST JOHN XIX (4–16)

[188]

REMBRANDT (1607–69)   *National Gallery, London*

("Christ Before Pilate")

CRUCIFY HIM!

JESUS' FAREWELL TO THE DAUGHTERS OF JERUSALEM

AND as they led him away, they laid hold upon one Simon, a Cyrenian, coming out of the country, and on him they laid the cross, that he might bear it after Jesus. And there followed him a great company of people, and of women, which also bewailed and lamented him. But Jesus turning unto them said:—"Daughters of Jerusalem, weep not for me, but weep for yourselves, and for your children. For, behold, the days are coming, in the which they shall say, Blessed are the barren, and the wombs that never bare, and the paps which never gave suck. Then shall they begin to say to the mountains, Fall on us; and to the hills, Cover us. For if they do these things in a green tree, what shall be done in the dry?" And there were also two other, malefactors, led with him to be put to death.

ST LUKE XXIII (26–32)

THE CRUCIFIXION

AND when they were come to the place, which is called Calvary, there they crucified him, and the malefactors, one on the right hand, and the other on the left.

ST LUKE XXIII (33)

TINTORETTO (1512–94)   *Scuola di S. Rocco, Venice*

THE CRUCIFIXION

THE INSCRIPTION ON THE CROSS AND THE PARTING OF
JESUS' GARMENTS

AND Pilate wrote a title, and put it on the cross. And the writing was:—

JESUS OF NAZARETH THE KING OF THE JEWS.

This title then read many of the Jews: for the place where Jesus was crucified was nigh to the city: and it was written in Hebrew, Greek, and Latin. Then said the chief priests of the Jews to Pilate:—"Write not, The King of the Jews; but that he said, I am King of the Jews." Pilate answered:—"What I have written I have written."

Then the soldiers, when they had crucified Jesus, took his garments, and made four parts, to every soldier a part; and also his coat: now the coat was without seam, woven from the top throughout. They said therefore among themselves:—"Let us not rend it, but cast lots for it, whose it shall be": that the scripture might be fulfilled, which saith:—They parted my raiment among them, And for my vesture they did cast lots. These things therefore the soldiers did.

ST JOHN XIX (19–24)

JESUS IS MOCKED

AND they that passed by railed on him, wagging their heads, and saying:— "Ah, thou that destroyest the temple, and buildest it in three days, save thyself, and come down from the cross." Likewise also the chief priests mocking said among themselves with the scribes:—"He saved others; himself he cannot save. Let Christ the King of Israel descend now from the cross, that we may see and believe."

ST MARK XV (29–32a)

BLAKE (1757–1827)

Collection of the late W. Graham Robertson, Esq.

THE SOLDIERS CASTING LOTS FOR CHRIST'S GARMENT

JESUS COMMENDS HIS MOTHER TO JOHN

NOW there stood by the cross of Jesus his mother, and his mother's sister, Mary the wife of Cleophas, and Mary Magdalene. When Jesus therefore saw his mother, and the disciple standing by, whom he loved, he saith unto his mother:—"Woman, behold thy son!" Then saith he to the disciple:—"Behold thy mother!" And from that hour that disciple took her unto his own home.

ST JOHN XIX (25–27)

THE THIEVES CRUCIFIED WITH JESUS

AND one of the malefactors which were hanged railed on him, saying:—"If thou be Christ, save thyself and us." But the other answering rebuked him, saying:—"Dost not thou fear God, seeing thou art in the same condemnation? And we indeed justly; for we receive the due reward of our deeds: but this man hath done nothing amiss." And he said unto Jesus:—"Lord, remember me when thou comest into thy kingdom." And Jesus said unto him:—"Verily I say unto thee, today shalt thou be with me in paradise."

ST LUKE XXIII (39–43)

JESUS DIES

AND when the sixth hour was come, there was darkness over the whole land until the ninth hour. And at the ninth hour Jesus cried with a loud voice, saying:—"Eloi, Eloi, lama sabachthani?" which is, being interpreted, My God My God, why hast thou forsaken me? And some of them that stood by, when they heard it, said:—"Behold, he calleth Elijah." And one ran and filled a spunge full of vinegar, and put it on a reed, and gave him to drink, saying:— "Let alone; let us see whether Elijah will come to take him down." And Jesus cried with a loud voice, and gave up the ghost. And the veil of the temple was rent in twain from the top to the bottom. And when the centurion, which stood over against him, saw that he so cried out, and gave up the ghost, he said:—"Truly this man was the Son of God." There were also women looking on afar off: among whom was Mary Magdalene, and Mary the mother of James the less and of Joses, and Salome; (who also, when he was in Galilee, followed him, and ministered unto him;) and many other women which came up with him unto Jerusalem.

ST MARK XV (33–41)

[194]

JOHN AND THE VIRGIN

JESUS' SIDE IS PIERCED

THE Jews therefore, because it was the preparation, that the bodies should not remain upon the cross on the sabbath day, (for that sabbath day was an high day,) besought Pilate that their legs might be broken, and that they might be taken away. Then came the soldiers, and brake the legs of the first, and of the other which was crucified with him. But when they came to Jesus, and saw that he was dead already, they brake not his legs: but one of the soldiers with a spear pierced his side, and forthwith came there out blood and water. And he that saw it bare record, and his record is true: and he knoweth that he saith true, that ye might believe. For these things were done, that the scripture should be fulfilled:—A bone of him shall not be broken. And again another scripture saith:—They shall look on him whom they pierced.

ST JOHN XIX (31–37)

JESUS IS BURIED

AND now when the even was come, because it was the preparation, that is, the day before the sabbath, Joseph of Arimathæa, an honourable counsellor, which also waited for the kingdom of God, came, and went in boldly unto Pilate, and craved the body of Jesus. And Pilate marvelled if he were already dead: and calling unto him the centurion, he asked him whether he had been any while dead. And when he knew it of the centurion, he gave the body to Joseph. And he bought fine linen, and took him down, and wrapped him in the linen, and laid him in a sepulchre which was hewn out of a rock, and rolled a stone unto the door of the sepulchre. And Mary Magdalene and Mary the mother of Joses beheld where he was laid.

ST MARK XV (42–47)

THE SEPULCHRE IS SEALED AND WATCHED

NOW the next day, that followed the day of the preparation, the chief priests and Pharisees came together unto Pilate, saying:—"Sir, we remember that that deceiver said, while he was yet alive, After three days I will rise again. Command therefore that the sepulchre be made sure until the third day, lest his disciples come by night, and steal him away, and say unto the people, he is risen from the dead: so the last error shall be worse than the first." Pilate said unto them:—"Ye have a watch: go your way, make it as sure as ye can." So they went, and made the sepulchre sure, sealing the stone, and setting a watch.

ST MATTHEW XXVII (62–66)

FRA ANGELICO (1387–1455)   *Courtesy of the National Gallery of Art, Washington, D.C. (Kress Collection)*

THE ENTOMBMENT

THE RESURRECTION

IN the end of the sabbath, as it began to dawn toward the first day of the week, came Mary Magdalene and the other Mary to see the sepulchre.

And, behold, there was a great earthquake: for the angel of the Lord descended from heaven, and came and rolled back the stone from the door, and sat upon it. His countenance was like lightning, and his raiment white as snow: and for fear of him the keepers did shake, and became as dead men. And the angel answered and said unto the women:—"Fear not ye: for I know that ye seek Jesus, which was crucified. He is not here: for he is risen, as he said. Come, see the place where the Lord lay. And go quickly, and tell his disciples that he is risen from the dead; and, behold, he goeth before you into Galilee; there shall ye see him: lo, I have told you." And they departed quickly from the sepulchre with fear and great joy; and did run to bring his disciples word.

ST MATTHEW XXVIII (1-8)

PETER RUNS TO THE SEPULCHRE

PETER therefore went forth, and that other disciple, and came to the sepulchre. So they ran both together: and the other disciple did outrun Peter, and came first to the sepulchre. And he stooping down, and looking in, saw the linen clothes lying; yet went he not in. Then cometh Simon Peter following him, and went into the sepulchre, and seeth the linen clothes lie, and the napkin, that was about his head, not lying with the linen clothes, but wrapped together in a place by itself. Then went in also that other disciple, which came first to the sepulchre, and he saw, and believed. For as yet they knew not the scripture, that he must rise again from the dead. Then the disciples went away again unto their own home.

ST JOHN XX (3-10)

[198]

AFTER P. BREUGHEL THE ELDER (c. 1525–69)   *From an anonymous engraving in the British Museum*

THE RESURRECTION

JESUS APPEARS TO MARY MAGDALENE

BUT Mary stood without at the selpulchre weeping: and as she wept, she stooped down, and looked into the sepulchre, and seeth two angels in white sitting, the one at the head, and the other at the feet, where the body of Jesus had lain. And they say unto her:—"Woman, why weepest thou?" She saith unto them:—"Because they have taken away my Lord, and I know not where they have laid him." And when she had thus said, she turned herself back, and saw Jesus standing, and knew not that it was Jesus. Jesus saith unto her:—"Woman, why weepest thou? whom seekest thou?" She, supposing him to be the gardener, saith unto him:—"Sir, if thou hast borne him hence, tell me where thou hast laid him, and I will take him away." Jesus saith unto her:—"Mary." She turned herself, and saith unto him:—"Rabboni"; which is to say, Master. Jesus saith unto her:—"Touch me not; for I am not yet ascended to my Father: but go to my brethren, and say unto them, I ascend unto my Father, and your Father; and to my God, and your God." Mary Magdalene came and told the disciples that she had seen the Lord, and that he had spoken these things unto her.

ST JOHN XX (11–18)

THE SOLDIERS TELL THE CHIEF PRIESTS

NOW when they were going, behold, some of the watch came into the city, and shewed unto the chief priests all the things that were done. And when they were assembled with the elders, and had taken counsel, they gave large money unto the soldiers, saying:—"Say ye, his disciples came by night, and stole him away while we slept. And if this come to the governor's ears, we will persuade him, and secure you." So they took the money, and did as they were taught: and this saying is commonly reported among the Jews until this day.

ST MATTHEW XXVIII (11–15)

HANS HOLBEIN THE YOUNGER (1497–1543) *Hampton Court Palace (reproduced by gracious permission of H.M. the King)*

TOUCH ME NOT

AND, behold, two of them went that same day to a village called Emmaus, which was from Jerusalem about threescore furlongs. And they talked together of all these things which had happened. And it came to pass, that, while they communed together and reasoned, Jesus himself drew near, and went with them. But their eyes were holden that they should not know him. And he said unto them:—"What manner of communications are these that ye have one to another, as ye walk, and are sad?" And the one of them, whose name was Cleopas, answering said unto him:—"Art thou only a stranger in Jerusalem, and hast not known the things which are come to pass there in these days?" And he said unto them:—"What things?" And they said unto him:—"Concerning Jesus of Nazareth, which was a prophet mighty in deed and word before God and all the people: and how the chief priests and our rulers delivered him to be condemned to death, and have crucified him. But we trusted that it had been he which should have redeemed Israel: and beside all this, to day is the third day since these things were done. Yea, and certain women also of our company made us astonished, which were early at the sepulchre: and when they found not his body, they came, saying, that they had also seen a vision of angels, which said that he was alive. And certain of them which were with us went to the sepulchre, and found it even so as the women had said: but him they saw not." Then he said unto them:—"O fools, and slow of heart to believe all that the prophets have spoken: ought not Christ to have suffered these things, and to enter into his glory?" And beginning at Moses and all the prophets, he expounded unto them in all the scriptures the things concerning himself. And they drew nigh unto the village, whither they went: and he made as though he would have gone further. But they constrained him, saying:—"Abide with us: for it is toward evening, and the day is far spent." And he went in to tarry with them. And it came to pass, as he sat at meat with them, he took bread, and blessed it, and brake, and gave to them. And their eyes were opened, and they knew him; and he vanished out of their sight. And they said one to another:—"Did not our heart burn within us, while he talked with us by the way, and while he opened to us the scriptures?"

And they rose up the same hour, and returned to Jerusalem, and found the eleven gathered together, and them that were with them, saying:—"The Lord is risen indeed, and hath appeared to Simon." And they told what things were done in the way, and how he was known of them in breaking of bread.

ST LUKE XXIV (13–35)

REMBRANDT (1607–69)

THE SUPPER AT EMMAUS

JESUS APPEARS TO THE DISCIPLES

THEN the same day at evening, being the first day of the week, when the doors were shut where the disciples were assembled for fear of the Jews, came Jesus and stood in the midst, and saith unto them:—"Peace be unto you." And when he had so said, he shewed unto them his hands and his side. Then were the disciples glad when they saw the Lord. Then said Jesus to them again:—"Peace be unto you: as my Father hath sent me, even so send I you." And when he had said this, he breathed on them, and saith unto them:— "Receive ye the Holy Ghost: whose soever sins ye remit, they are remitted unto them; and whose soever sins ye retain, they are retained." But Thomas, one of the twelve, called Didymus, was not with them when Jesus came. The other disciples therefore said unto him:—"We have seen the Lord." But he said unto them:—"Except I shall see in his hands the print of the nails, and put my finger into the print of the nails, and thrust my hand into his side, I will not believe."

ST JOHN XX (19–25)

JESUS APPEARS TO THOMAS

AND after eight days again his disciples were within, and Thomas with them: then came Jesus, the doors being shut, and stood in the midst, and said:— "Peace be unto you." Then saith he to Thomas:—"Reach hither thy finger, and behold my hands; and reach hither thy hand, and thrust it into my side: and be not faithless, but believing." And Thomas answered and said unto him:—"My Lord and my God." Jesus saith unto him:—"Thomas, because thou hast seen me, thou hast believed: blessed are they that have not seen, and yet have believed."

And many other signs truly did Jesus in the presence of his disciples, which are not written in this book: but these are written, that ye might believe that Jesus is the Christ, the Son of God; and that believing ye might have life through his name.

ST JOHN XX (26–31)

DUCCIO (c. 1260–c. 1340)   *Opera del Duomo, Siena*

JESUS APPEARING TO THE DISCIPLES

HANS BALDUNG GRIEN   *Kunstmuseum, Basel*
(c. 1480–c. 1545)
(A detail from "The Crucifixion of Christ")

MY LORD AND MY GOD!

AFTER these things Jesus shewed himself again to the disciples at the sea of Tiberias; and on this wise shewed he himself. There were together Simon Peter, and Thomas called Didymus, and Nathanael of Cana in Galilee, and the sons of Zebedee, and two other of his disciples. Simon Peter saith unto them:—"I go a fishing." They say unto him:—"We also go with thee." They went forth, and entered into a ship immediately; and that night they caught nothing. But when the morning was now come, Jesus stood on the shore: but the disciples knew not that it was Jesus. Then Jesus saith unto them:—"Children, have ye any meat?" They answered him, "No." And he said unto them:—"Cast the net on the right side of the ship and ye shall find." They cast therefore, and now they were not able to draw it for the multitude of fishes. Therefore that disciple whom Jesus loved saith unto Peter:—"It is the Lord." Now when Simon Peter heard that it was the Lord, he girt his fisher's coat unto him, (for he was naked) and did cast himself into the sea. And the other disciples came in a little ship; (for they were not far from land, but as it were two hundred cubits,) dragging the net with fishes. As soon then as they were come to land, they saw a fire of coals there, and fish laid thereon, and bread. Jesus saith unto them:—"Bring of the fish which ye have now caught." Simon Peter went up, and drew the net to land full of great fishes, an hundred and fifty and three: and for all there were so many, yet was not the net broken. Jesus saith unto them:—"Come and dine." And none of the disciples durst ask him:—"Who art thou?" knowing that it was the Lord. Jesus then cometh, and taketh bread, and giveth them, and fish likewise. This is now the third time that Jesus shewed himself to his disciples, after that he was risen from the dead.

ST JOHN XXI (1–14)

KONRAD WITZ (First half of XV Century)　　　　　　　　　　　　　　　　　Musée d'Art et d'Histoire, Geneva

("The Miraculous Draught of Fishes")

IT IS THE LORD!

so when they had dined, Jesus saith to Simon Peter:—"Simon, son of Jonas, lovest thou me more than these?" He saith unto him:—"Yea, Lord; thou knowest that I love thee." He saith unto him:—"Feed my lambs." He saith to him again the second time:—"Simon, son of Jonas, lovest thou me?" He saith unto him:—"Yea, Lord; thou knowest that I love thee." He saith unto him:—"Feed my sheep." He saith unto him the third time:—"Simon, son of Jonas, lovest thou me?" Peter was grieved because he said unto him the third time, Lovest thou me? And he said unto him:—"Lord, thou knowest all things; thou knowest that I love thee." Jesus saith unto him:—"Feed My sheep. Verily, verily, I say unto thee, when thou wast young, thou girdedst thyself, and walkedst whither thou wouldest: but when thou shalt be old, thou shalt stretch forth thy hands, and another shall gird three, and carry thee whither thou wouldest not." This spake he, signifying by what death he should glorify God. And when he had spoken this, he saith unto him:—"Follow me." Then Peter, turning about, seeth the disciple whom Jesus loved following; which also leaned on his breast at supper, and said, Lord, which is he that betrayeth thee? Peter seeing him saith to Jesus:—"Lord, and what shall this man do?" Jesus saith unto him:—"If I will that he tarry till I come, what is that to thee? follow thou me." Then went this saying abroad among the brethren, that that disciple should not die: yet Jesus said not unto him:—"He shall not die"; but "If I will that he tarry till I come, what is that to thee?"

This is the disciple which testifieth of these things, and wrote these things: and we know that his testimony is true.

ST JOHN XXI (15–24)

RUBENS (1577–1640)

("Christ's Charge to Peter")

Wallace Collection, London

FEED MY LAMBS

JESUS APPEARS ON THE MOUNTAIN IN GALILEE

THEN the eleven disciples went away into Galilee, into a mountain where Jesus had appointed them. And when they saw him, they worshipped him: but some doubted. And Jesus came and spake unto them, saying:—"All power is given unto me in heaven and in earth. Go ye therefore, and teach all nations, baptizing them in the name of the Father, and of the Son, and of the Holy Ghost; teaching them to observe all things whatsoever I have commanded you: and, lo, I am with you alway, even unto the end of the world."

ST MATTHEW XXVIII (16–20)

THE ASCENSION

AND he said unto them:—"These are the words which I spake unto you, while I was yet with you, that all things must be fulfilled, which were written in the law of Moses, and in the prophets, and in the psalms, concerning me." Then opened he their understanding, that they might understand the scriptures, and said unto them:—"Thus it is written, and thus it behoved Christ to suffer, and to rise from the dead the third day: and that repentance and remission of sins should be preached in his name among all nations, beginning at Jerusalem. And ye are witnesses of these things. And, behold, I send the promise of my Father upon you: but tarry ye in the city of Jerusalem, until ye be endued with power from on high." And he led them out as far as to Bethany, and he lifted up his hands, and blessed them. And it came to pass, while He blessed them, he was parted from them, and carried up into heaven. And they worshipped him, and returned to Jerusalem with great joy: and were continually in the temple, praising and blessing God.

ST LUKE XXIV (44–53)

MANTEGNA (1431–1506)

THE ASCENSION

DIERIC BOUTS (1400?–75)

Boymans Museum, Rotterdam

JOHN ON PATMOS

AND there are also many other things which Jesus
did, the which, if they should be written every
one, I suppose that even the world itself could not
contain the books that should be written. Amen.

ST JOHN XXI (25)